TREASURES *of* DARKNESS

Copyright © 2014, Jane Johnson Photography & Design, LLC
All rights reserved.
ISBN-13: 978-0692258187 • ISBN-10: 0692258183

Unless otherwise stated, all Scripture citations are from the NKJV © 1994 by Thomas Nelson, Inc.
Cover design by Jane Johnson Design
Cover photograph by Jenna Michelle Photography

HELLO & WELCOME

Thank you so much for being here. For embarking on a brand new journey with me. For being brave and open and hungering for more of Him.

The words on these pages are the result of a dish cloth of faith being wrung dry. They are straight out of my prayer journal. Real. Raw. Honest. More honest and vulnerable than I have been outside of conversations with Him ... ever. Which is scary for me. But glory for Him.

I wrote this study in 2011. It's nine weeks long, with five days of homework for each week. A God-breathed, Holy-Spirit-inspired, I-could-never-have-done-this-if-it-wasn't-for-Him type of study. We were five years into our wait for a family. My best friend was five months into an 18-month battle with stage four cancer - a battle she lost one year later. I was neck-deep in heartache. *Words rang hollow in my heart pierced by pain.*[1]

But through the plucking of my heartstrings came this. The book you're holding in your hands. Cover uncreased. Pages fresh. Treasures undiscovered.

It's such an honor to have you here with me.

Truly.

Praying His Spirit fills you with every word,

---

[1] Ray Stedman, *Let God Be God*

SMALL STEPS

Generally, a book's forward is written by a published author or person of significance. I am neither. I am a completely ordinary person by almost any standard. The one *extra*ordinary thing that qualifies me to write this is that this study, and it's author, has deeply affected my walk with God.

I write this coming out the other side of my own well-wrung dish cloth experience. A little over a year ago I got *that call* from my father's doctor. The next day I sat across a rustic restaurant table from Jane, explaining how I would be moving home for the rest of the year to care for him.

The following week I found myself saying goodbye. Jane stood beside me, still very much aching from her own pain. There we began a year together unlike any I'll ever again experience. She stood in front of me, guiding the way through a difficult path. I stood beside her, listening and asking the difficult questions.

A year later I sat across a rustic restaurant table from Jane as she counted the weeks left until she and her husband were to move on to an adventure years in the making. There were nine. She paused, and asked me a question she already knew the answer to. The next afternoon she sent an email to a group of women asking if they'd walk beside her through a rough, unedited nine-week bible study she had been sitting on.

He couldn't have woven the fabric of women together with a thread more of perfection. Struggling with divorce, infertility, death, guilt, inadequacy and grief, this band of women came together in Jane's living room every week, and together combated years of spiritual and physical pain. Nine weeks later we were different. Better. Changed.

I pray you discover abundant healing. I pray He reveals abundant love. I pray you stick through the study – especially when you feel you cannot. For me, that is when He revealed His hidden treasures. Even through the darkness.

- Amanda Lenke

WHAT YOU WILL NEED

The following items are recommended to have on hand in order
to get the most out of our study together:

1. Bible (I use the NKJV unless otherwise noted)

2. Journal (to record the verses and pray through the homework)

3. Computer (you will be on www.blueletterbible.org every day)

This study not only provides a truth-trail of the things He has taught me through a season of suffering and loss, it also teaches how to dig into Scripture on your own, through any season.

Hang on tight; you're about to jump into the deep end of the study-Scripture pool!

When the people of the land come before the LORD on the appointed feast days, whoever enters by way of the north gate to worship shall go out by way of the south gate; and whoever enters by way of the south gate shall go out by way of the north gate.

He shall not return by way of the gate through which he came.

Ezekiel 46:9

BEFORE WE BEGIN...

Where are you, right this moment, with the LORD? What does your faith look like? What do you want Him to do in these next nine weeks? How do you want to leave this study changed? Take a minute to pray and invite His Spirit into this journey.

I will give you the

TREASURES *of* DARKNESS

*and hidden riches of secret places
that you may know that I, the LORD, Who call you
by your name, am the God of Israel.*

Isaiah 45:3

THE BACKGROUND
journal pieces and other things

It was late summer in 2011 and I had just begun reading a new book. *Let God be God: Life-Changing Truths from the Book of Job* by Ray Stedman - one of the twentieth century's foremost pastors and biblical expositors. Just a few pages in, my heart began to be convicted. Everything was taken from Job. *Everything.* Yet he didn't complain. He didn't blame God. He didn't question Him or say "why did this happen to me? This is so unfair!" The pages in my journal were full of wrestling. And questioning. And raw emotion. I wish I could have responded like Job had to difficult circumstances. But I was also incredibly thankful that God knows my heart. And He is patient with my emotions.

Up to that point, my year had been a circle of hope, discouragement, thankfulness, hope again, fear of hope, thankfulness...it was an exercise in endurance. And I happened to be on the discouragement side of the circle. Another month. Another period. Another ugly cry in the closet. Followed by another pull-myself-up-by-the-bootstraps-and-pour-it-out-to-Him-again morning.

(8:20am) Saturday   8/20/11

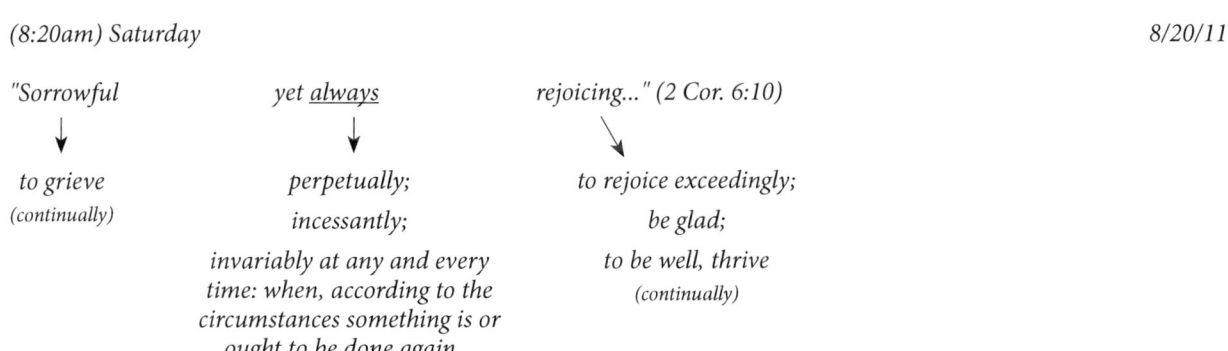

I cried in the closet last night. Again. I tucked myself into the back, dark corner and really let out. Even asking for the joy in the morning because I'm tired of the weeping. I let myself hope again. Sort of a last ditch effort. I hoped for a positive pregnancy test today. And it isn't so...and I cried. This is the moment I was reading about on Thursday. The moment I want to stop running the race. Stop hoping. Stop weaving my robes. And yet I push through the tears, because hope does <u>not</u> disappoint. I know continual sorrow. LORD help me to also know the gladness and joyful cries. Help me to perpetually, incessantly rejoice. To thrive. To throw my thread beautifully and confidently. When, according to the circumstances, I should cry again ... help me to rejoice.

Four months later, I opened *Streams in the Desert* (my favorite devotional) on a Tuesday morning. It was based on Isaiah 45:3. *"I will give you the treasures of darkness and hidden riches of secret places that you may know that I, the LORD, Who call you by your name, am the God of Israel. "* And this story followed:

"In the famous lace shops of Brussels, there are certain rooms devoted to the spinning of the finest and most delicate patterns. These rooms are altogether darkened, save for a light from one very small window, which falls directly upon the pattern. There is only one spinner in the room, and he sits where the narrow stream of light falls upon the threads

of his weaving. 'Thus,' we are told by the guide, 'do we secure our choicest products. Lace is always more delicately and beautifully woven when the worker himself is in the dark and only his pattern is in the light.'" [1]

Verse three, and the story that followed, simultaneously spoke to me and intrigued me. I began to dig. And I learned that it was a prophecy about Cyrus, the renowned 6th century King of Persia, given nearly 200 years before he was actually born. A prophecy that brought Israel out of their harrowing captivity in Babylon and back home to the land of promise. Verse three refers to the rich treasures of Babylon that the kings had taken as spoils of war from everyone they encountered - especially the Israelites. They were shoved away and locked up for many years or buried underground, never seeing the light of day.

Historical documents say that Cyrus obtained thirty-four thousand pounds weight of gold and five hundred thousand talents of silver from the conquest of Asia. In modern day values, that would add up to nearly $800,000,000! Incredible riches came out of heartbreaking captivity. Just like God promised. There *are* treasures in the darkness. Invaluable, faith-changing, treasures. Through the cancer. The unanswered prayer. The sorrow. And the pain. If we just dig a little deeper. Press in a little further. He's waiting with treasures to balance the pain by His grace piled high with mercy and truth. That we may know that He, the LORD, Who calls us by our names, is the God of Israel. He waits. With treasures in hand.

The devotional ended this way: *"Sometimes [our weaving is in the] dark. We cannot understand what we are doing. We do not see the web we are weaving. We are not able to discover any beauty, any possible good in our experience. Yet if we are faithful and fail not and faint not, we shall some day know that the most exquisite work of all our life was done in those days when it was so dark."* [2]

---

1   *Streams in the Desert - December 13th*

THIS WEEK'S NUGGET:

Let no corrupt word proceed out of your mouth, but what is good for necessary edification, that it may impart grace to the hearers. And do not grieve the Holy Spirit of God, by whom you were sealed for the day of redemption. Let all bitterness, wrath, anger, clamour, and evil speaking be put away from you, with all malice

And be kind to one another, tenderhearted, forgiving one another, even as God in Christ forgave you.

Ephesians 4:29-32

TREASURES *of* DARKNESS

WEEK 1: TAMING THE TONGUE

- INTRODUCTION -

The summer after my best friend Shawna was diagnosed, I was studying the book of Job. Really studying it. In depth. Simultaneously dissecting commentaries, looking up the original Hebrew definitions, and reading collections of sermons dedicated to the book. In the week leading up to writing the first week of this study, I was struck by these words:

"Surely God will never do wickedly, nor will the Almighty pervert justice. Who gave Him charge over the earth? Or who appointed Him over the whole world? If He should set His heart on it, if He should gather to Himself His Spirit and His breath, all flesh would perish together, and man would return to dust." (Job 34:12-15)

And I began to think.

If I can't breathe, I can't talk. The only reason I have breath is because He has given it to me.

And the verses came flooding.

"In (Your) hand is the life of every living thing, and the breath of all mankind." (Job 12:10)

"As long as my breath is in me, and the breath of God in my nostrils, my lips will not speak wickedness." (Job 27:3-4)

"The Spirit of God has made me, and the breath of the Almighty gives me life." (Job 33:4)

The Hebrew word for breath in this particular context is *něshamah*. It means breath, spirit - (a) the Spirit of God (imparting life and wisdom); (b) the spirit of man, soul.[1]

*"And the LORD God formed man of the dust of the ground and **breathed** into his nostrils the breath of life; and man became a living being." (Genesis 2:7)*

As I read the words, a beautiful picture formed: God bent over Adam, blowing life into His otherwise breathless piece of art. Without missing a beat, Adam takes up the rhythm of His breathing. His life-giving breathing. In. And out. And in. And out. *How can I possibly use my breath to complain about the life He has given me? The plan He has laid out for me? My breath is not my own. Just like my life is not my own.* <u>Whatever</u> *He chooses to give (or withold) is a gift. And*

---

[1] Old Testament Hebrew Lexicon, Strong's H5397

my only responsibility is to say as Job did: 'Blessed be the name of the LORD.' (Job 1:21)

With that in mind, read James 3: 2, 8: "...we all stumble in many things. If anyone does not stumble in word, he is a perfect man, able also to bridle the whole body...but no man can tame the tongue. It is an unruly evil, full of deadly poison."

I'd like you to read a handful of different translations of the same section of Scripture to get a fuller picture of what James is trying to say:

"If you could find someone whose speech was perfectly true, you'd have a perfect person, in perfect control of life. This is scary: You can tame a tiger, but you can't tame a tongue—it's never been done. The tongue runs wild, a wanton killer. With our tongues we bless God our Father; with the same tongues we curse the very men and women he made in his image. Curses and blessings out of the same mouth!" (James 3:2, 8 - The Message)

"For we all often stumble and fall and offend in many things. And if anyone does not offend in speech [never says the wrong things], he is a fully developed character and a perfect man, able to control his whole body and to curb his entire nature." (James 3:2, 8 - Amplified Version)

"If we could control our tongues, we would be perfect and could also control ourselves in every other way." (James 3:2 - New Living Translation)

There is not one person on this earth that can tame their tongue. And if no one can successfully restrain their tongue for good to the point that they will never again struggle with gossip, slander, or simply saying the wrong thing, how much more do we need to actively and continually pray that we can at least make it through one day successfully?

We need to knowingly use our breath, as much as is within our abilities, to honor and glorify God.

LORD, help me to feel the cadence of Your breathing with every breath I take today. Remind me that my breath is not my own and show me ways that I'm not using it to best glorify You. Retrain my mind, and my breath, LORD.

TREASURES of DARKNESS

WEEK 1: TAMING THE TONGUE

- DAY 1 -

Read Ephesians 4:29-32, and then write it in your journal. You will be studying each individual verse this week.

Now you're about to jump into the deep end. Get on your computer. Go to www.blueletterbible.org and put Ephesians 4:29 in the search box. Click on the "tools" button to the left of the verse to show the Greek Lexicon (a dictionary that was created for a deeper understanding of the original text of the Greek Old and New Testament). In the second column of the tools window, you will see a list of numbers associated with each word or phrase. Those are the numbers assigned to the corresponding Greek from the Strong's concordance of Biblical words. Click on the Strong's number next to each of the following words and write down their definitions (called Outline of Biblical Usage on the website):

Corrupt: _____
_____

One of the cross-references for this particular word is Matthew 12:33 where it's translated "bad fruit". Go read it.

What is a tree known for? _____

If you study the gospels, you'll notice a very simple truth repeated about trees and their fruit. Take a minute to read both Matthew 7:17-18 and Luke 6:43.

If we break this idea of corrupt words down into the simplest of black and white terms, it's safe to assume that corrupt words are equal to bad fruit. And a good tree does not bear bad fruit. Ever. One bad piece of fruit makes for a bad tree. It affects the full tree. Not just part of it.

I don't know a lot about horticulture. Ok, I don't know anything about it. But I get the idea that the bad fruit grows as a result of something diseased within the tree. It's the visual result of what's happening inside. Just like a cancer patient's hair loss is the visual result of the poison inside their body trying to kill the rogue cancer cells.

Matthew 12:34 goes further to say "out of the abundance of the heart the mouth speaks". By the time the negative words reach your mouth, it's pretty safe to say that you're already consumed with some level of bitterness or resentment in your heart. Eventually, the bitterness has nowhere else to go but out. And the good tree produces a bad piece of fruit? No. The good tree produces one isolated little sickly branch? No. The bad fruit comes from a bad tree. *LORD, I long to be a healthy tree. A good tree.* Since we're at it, look up Matthew 12:33 in blueletterbible.org, and click on the Greek Lexicon word for "good". Write the very first word of the definition here: _____

The more good, wholesome, and edifying words come out of our mouths, the more beautiful we are. And we'd be lying if we didn't say that as women, we want to be beautiful. Inside and out. Go back to Ephesians 4:29 on blueletterbible.org and write down the Greek Lexicon definition for "good" (note: this is a different "good" than what you just looked up in Matthew): _____
_____
_____
_____

If you scroll down on the page, you'll see a section called Thayer's Greek Lexicon which contains a lengthy paragraph describing all the different ways this particular word is used in the Greek language. Buried in the middle of the paragraph is a cross-reference to Acts 23:1, where Paul is talking about living in "good conscience before God until this day."

How often have you found yourself subconsciously looking over your shoulder before saying something to make sure the person in reference doesn't happen to be within ear shot? Or you've said something and later regretted it?

One of the definitions of "good" in Ephesians 4:29 is a peaceful conscience.

Write down the Greek definition for "edifying": _____
_____
_____
_____

I was struck by the idea of only allowing words to proceed out of my mouth that promote another's holiness. Just chew on that for a second. Edification also means the process of building up. The Thayer's Lexicon explains it in reference to "the heavenly body, the abode of the soul after death (2 Corinthians 5:1)". Do my words provide a golden, holy brick that helps the hearer build their "treasure in heaven"? Or is it robbing them of their treasure?

Finally, write down the Greek definition for "grace": _____
_____
_____

A spoken, edifying word gives grace to the hearer when God uses it as His instrument. When we slander and gossip, we aren't giving God the opportunity to speak through us. Now, what do you do with all this information?

Turn Ephesians 4:29 into a prayer in your journal. Don't just recite the verse. Really pray it. Make it personal. Ask for forgiveness if you need to, and be specific. Talk with God specifically about the things that struck you most as you studied these words. And pray for His grace to be able to promote the holiness of those around you.

TREASURES *of* DARKNESS

WEEK 1: TAMING THE TONGUE

- DAY 2 -

Read Ephesians 4:29-30. Write verse 30 in your journal.

Now that we know what we know from yesterday's digging, we're going to be held accountable. We have a choice to make as to whether or not we will diligently and proactively work toward not letting any corrupt word proceed out of our mouths.

Read Isaiah 61:1-3.

Isaiah is proclaiming what God has called him to do. And He's being very specific in speaking the things that God wants to do for the Israelites. If they would just let Him.

Now skip ahead two chapters and read Isaiah 63:9-10.

God never forces His will upon us. And because of that, the Israelites had a choice to make. God is always standing by ready and waiting to take all these burdens and replace them with good things. And throughout the Old Testament, we see the Israelites consistently choosing God for a time, then setting Him aside for awhile.

The amplified version of Isaiah 64:10 says this: *"But they rebelled and grieved (actively resisting) His Holy Spirit..."*

What happened when they grieved His Holy Spirit: _____
_____
_____

Our introduction to this week discusses the impossibility of taming the tongue. Thankfully God specializes in making the impossible possible. The idea of taming our tongue is just a small example of the larger picture. The other struggles. God is standing by to equip us with the supernatural ability to promote holiness. We just have to choose to accept it.

And when we don't...His Spirit is grieved.

What does it really mean to grieve the Spirit of God? Go back to blueletterbible.org and search for Isaiah 63:10. Before you actually click on any of the words, take note of the far right column titled "Parsing". A lot of times, there is more than one definition for a word. If there is a button in the parsing column, you will be directed to the correct definition. In this particular case, the parsing link instructs you to look for the Piel stem, which is an intensive action. You'll see that clearly when you read the definition. Click on the Strong's link next to "grieve" and look for the section titled Piel in the Outline of Biblical Usage. There's a much stronger word that can be used for "grieve". What is it? _____

If you read the Gesenius' Hebrew-Chaldee Lexicon description below, there's a much more interesting picture given in the first reference. What is it? _____
_____
_____
_____

"The original idea is perhaps that of cutting..." That struck me. Because as soon as I read it, I thought of one thing - particularly since this is the Old Testament: creating idols.

The second we resist the Spirit of God, we're actively choosing to develop and form the very idols that separate us from Him. The second Piel definition means to shape or to form. Grieving the Spirit of God cuts apart what He is wanting to do, and we begin forming our own choices. Our own self-interest. Our own idols.

Go back to Ephesians 4:30 and read the verse again.

Now that we know the definition of grieving the Spirit of God from the Old Testament, the idea of being sealed for the day of redemption is a little bit more intriguing.

Read Ephesians 1:13. Once we believed unto salvation, what were we sealed with?
_____
_____

The Spirit *Himself* is the seal of our redemption. We were sealed by the Spirit and with the Spirit. And when we grieve the Spirit, according to Isaiah, we're performing an act of cutting. The only thing that's really destructive to a seal is cutting. When we actively resist the Spirit, and choose to do what we know we shouldn't do, we're essentially trying to cut open the seal of our own redemption. How convicting is that?

What are areas in your life beyond the tongue that you suspect might be grieving the Spirit?
_____
_____
_____
_____

Turn all the things you've learned today into a prayer in your journal. Take your time. Allow Him to show areas in your own life where you're grieving Him (and may not even realize it). And then thank Him that we are sealed for the day of redemption.

TREASURES *of* DARKNESS

WEEK 1: TAMING THE TONGUE

- DAY 3 -

Read Ephesians 4:29-31. Write verse 31 in your journal.

Let's get right into it - go to www.blueletterbible.org and search for verse 31.

Click on the Strong's number next to each of the following words and write down their definitions:

Bitterness: _____
_____

Did you notice the definition next to the letter "b"? *"A bitter root, and so producing a bitter fruit."* Think back on your homework for Day 1, particularly the part about good trees vs. bad trees. We've been talking all week about taming the tongue, and now we're going to start looking at the steps we can actually take to do that.

By the time we begin speaking corrupt words, a bitter root has long since been growing in us that produces the words that result. Bitterness is a tricky, sneaky little thing that easily overtakes us without us realizing it. A misconception or a perceived wrong can quickly spiral out of control. Once we get bitterness in our hearts, it's very difficult to get it out. And it doesn't poison anyone but ourselves.

Read Hebrews 12:14-15.

Pursue peace with all people. Actively. Looking carefully for any root of bitterness that causes trouble, and defiles many. Because bitter roots produce bitter fruit. And for some reason, we're more apt to share our bitter fruit with anyone that will take it than our good fruit.

Flip over to Deuteronomy 29:18, paying particular attention to the last part of the verse. I did a quick read about wormwood on wikipedia, and found this little tidbit interesting: "it is used in companion planting to suppress weeds, because its roots secrete substances that inhibit the growth of surrounding plants".

Did you catch that? *Wormwood inhibits the growth of surrounding plants.* Remember what you just read in Hebrews 12? Bitterness defiles many. And when people are defiled, their spiritual growth is *inhibited*.

Read Exodus 15:22-26.

Now we get to the good part. The Israelites had been wandering in the wilderness and were without any water for three solid days. When they finally found water, it was undrinkable. They were furious. They were bitter at Moses, perceiving that he misled them. And they told him about it. And he told God about it. And God told Moses what to do about it.

How did God heal the bitter waters? Write verse 25 here: _____
_____
_____
_____
_____
_____

At the end of verse 26, God introduces a new piece of His character by revealing another name of His to the Israelites: Jehovah Rapha. The LORD Who Heals You. He made the introduction by demonstrating His power over the most common disease His people suffer from across the board: bitterness.

The only way we can heal the bitterness in our hearts is to throw it upon a tree (also translated wood). But not just any wood. It must be the wood of the cross. And then we have to leave it there. Because as long as the tree was in the bitter water at Marah, the water was made sweet. The verses say nothing of the tree being removed. I imagine that if the tree were taken out, the water would go back to where it was. Maybe not immediately, but over time whatever was in the tree that sweetened the waters would fade. And the bitterness would slowly return to where it was. We have to be so careful to guard against bitterness because it's one of those things that just keeps coming back if we let it.

Go back to Ephesians 4. Look up the definition for "be put away".

You'll see quite a list of different translations. In these cases, I dig through the Thayer's Greek Lexicon until I find a reference to the particular verse I'm studying (which may or may not be there). On this word, you'll see it in the middle of the paragraph:

"*To rend away, to cut off, John 15:2.*" Look up John 15:2 and write it here: _____
_____
_____

It's time to think about any bitterness that you need to let the cross be cast into and allow the Vinedresser to remove. (Or something that is small now, but can easily turn into bitterness.) Take some time to turn the verses you've read today into prayers in your journal. Pray specifically. And rend away anything that Satan can turn into a bitter root. Because by it many are defiled.

TREASURES *of* DARKNESS

WEEK 1: TAMING THE TONGUE

- DAY 4 -

Read Ephesians 4:29-32. Write verse 32 in your journal.

Go to blueletterbible.org and look up the Strong's definition for "kind". If you read further in the Thayer's Greek Lexicon, you will see that the correct translation for this particular verse is the second one. Write it here:

_____
_____
_____

To be manageable is the opposite of harsh, hard, sharp, and bitter. When we are finally able to put the bitterness that we studied yesterday away from us, all that's left is kindness. I find it interesting that the root word of chrēstos means to grant a loan. To lend. The act of giving is rooted in kindness. There's a reason why giving gifts is a love language. If you're angry or bitter with someone, the last thing you want to do is give them a gift.

A pastor shared a handful of years ago about how he puts quite a bit of thought into buying someone a book if he's particularly frustrated with them, or their relationship is at odds. He said that it always dissipates the situation for him. That is a very specific example of this verse being acted out. He illustrated making the choice to put away the bitterness and, instead, choose kindness. Then acts it out through a gift of something that he loves.

Go back to blueletterbible.org and look up the Greek Lexicon for "tenderhearted":

_____
_____
_____

This definition surprised me. Strong bowels? What do your bowels have anything to do with being tenderhearted? And if you're tender, how can you be strong? As I dug more into it, I learned that the term bowels doesn't just refer to your intestines, it also includes your vital organs like the heart, lungs, and liver.

I think it's safe to say that we can replace "tenderhearted" with strong-hearted. It's interesting how the stronger you love someone, the more tender you are towards them. And how much more quickly you are moved to have compassion for them.

"...forgiving one another even as God in Christ forgave you."

I read a quote by Jamieson, Fauuset and Brown in their verse-by-verse expositional commentary on this verse and was so convicted at how simply, yet pointedly, they explained those words: *"It is but just that you in turn shall be so to your fellow men, who have not erred against you in the degree that you have erred against God."*

Yikes.

It doesn't matter what someone did. Or said. Or how they acted. Or what was perceived. It is still not to the same degree as our sin. And if God freely forgives me...how can I cling to bitterness, refusing to forgive those around me?

Matthew Henry was an English ministrer in the 17th century, and his commentary on scripture is one of my very favorites. He says this about the same passage:

"Occasions of difference will happen among Christ's disciples; and therefore they must be placable, and ready to forgive, therein resembling God Himself, who for Christ's sake hath forgiven them, and that more than they can forgive one another. Note, with God there is forgiveness; and He forgives sin for the sake of Jesus Christ, and on account of that atonement which He has made to divine justice. Note again, those who are forgiven of God should be of a forgiving spirit, and should forgive even as God forgives, sincerely and heartily, readily and cheerfully, universally and for ever, upon the sinner's sincere repentance, as remembering that they pray: forgive us our trespasses, as we forgive those who trespass against us."

I want you to just chew on these things. Spend some time praying in your journal over any unforgiveness you're harboring. Ask God to reveal any areas of unforgiveness in your life that you might not be aware of. And then start the prayer journey of letting go.

If you're not harboring any unforgiveness, spend time praying for the supernatural ability to be kind. Strong-hearted. Genuinely loving and compassionate to those around you. That might even mean specifically praying for your marriage, and for extra kindness toward your husband. Let God lead this time for you. Spend at least 15 minutes praying and/or waiting on the LORD.

TREASURES *of* DARKNESS

WEEK 1: TAMING THE TONGUE

- DAY 5 -

Read Ephesians 4:29-32 for the last time this week, and write all four verses in your journal.

I was hesitant to delve into the topic of unforgiveness, because I want to make sure we're going through things that are personally relevant to you. Ironically, I kept forgetting where we started in James last week. *No one* can tame the tongue. And the more I studied bitterness and unforgiveness, the more I realized just how relevant it is to all of us.

In her book *Praying God's Word*, Beth Moore puts it this way in the chapter on Overcoming Unforgiveness:

"No matter how different the rest of our challenges may be, every believer can count on a multitude of challenges to forgive. Remember, God's primary agenda in the life of a believer is to conform the child into the likeness of His Son, Jesus Christ. No other word sums up His character in relationship to use like the word forgiving. We never look more like Christ than when we forgive; since that's God's goal, we're destined for plenty of opportunities!"

She goes on to say, *"if only we could understand that God's unrelenting insistence on our forgiveness is for our own sakes, not the sake of the one who hurt us. God is faithful. He will plead our case and take up our cause... but only when we make a deliberate decision to cease representing ourselves in the matter."*

Confirming what we've already been studying this week, she explains: *"Innumerable strongholds are connected to an unwillingness to forgive. Left untreated, unforgiveness becomes spiritual cancer. Bitterness takes root, and since the root feeds the rest of the tree, every branch of our lives and every fruit on each limb ultimately become poisoned. Beloved sister, the bottom line is... unforgiveness makes us sick. Always spiritually. Often emotionally. And, surprisingly often, physically.*

"Please keep in mind that forgiveness is not defined by a feeling, although it will ultimately change our feelings. The Greek word most often translated "forgiveness" in New Testament Scripture is aphiemi, meaning 'to send forth or away, let go from oneself. To let go from one's power, possession. To let go from one's further... attendance, occupancy.' Forgiveness is our determined and deliberate willingness to let something go. To release it from our possession. To be willing and ready for it to no longer occupy us." And to let it go *to God.*

I've pulled a few of the scripture-prayers she included in the chapter. There's plenty more where this came from - if you would like them, you can find the book on Beth Moore's website[1] or at most Christian book stores.

---

[1] www.lproof.org

Lord, as hard as this may be for me to comprehend or rationalize, Your Word is clear: if I forgive others when they sin against me, You, my heavenly Father will also forgive me. (Matt. 6:14)

Lord God, if I do not forgive others their sins, You, my Father, will not forgive my sins. (Matt. 6:15)

Father, according to Your Word, if I judge others, I too will be judged, and with the same measure I use, it will be measured to me. (Matt. 7:1-2)

Christ Jesus, when I want so badly to judge, condemn, or refuse forgiveness to another person, I can hear Your Word speak to my heart saying, 'If you are without sin, be the first to throw a stone at them.' (John 8:7) I am *not* without sin. If I claim to be without sin, I deceive myself and the truth is not in me. (1 John 1:8)

Lord, I must ask myself why I look at the speck of sawdust in another person's eye and pay no attention to the plank in my own eye. How can I say to my brother, 'Let me take the speck out of your eye,' when all the time there is a plank in my own eye? O God, rescue me from being a hypocrite! Give me the honesty and courage to first take the plank out of my own eye, and then I may see clearly to remove the speck from another person's eye. (Matt. 7:3-5)

Jesus, in the parable of the unmerciful servant, the only person in the end who was imprisoned and tortured was the one who would not forgive. (Matt. 18:33-34) Help me to see the monumental price of unforgiveness. It is so enslaving and torturous. According to Matthew 18:35, You may allow me to suffer the same kind of repercussions if I refuse to forgive from my heart someone who has sinned against me.

Lord, Your Word tells me that when I stand praying, if I hold anything against anyone, I am to forgive him or her so that You, my Father in heaven, may forgive me my sins. (Mark 11:25)

God, if I am offering my gifts to You through worship or service and remember that my brother has something against me, I am to leave my gift there in front of the altar. I am to first go and be reconciled to my brother, then I am to come and offer my gift. (Matt. 5:23-24) Help me to be obedient to Your will.

If I do not judge, I will not be judged. If I do not condemn, I will not be condemned. If I forgive, I will be forgiven. (Luke 6:37) Help me, Lord, to extend more grace, and I will continue to receive more grace!

Lord Jesus, when You were being led out to be executed, after being beaten, ridiculed, and spit upon, You said, "Father, forgive them, for they do not know what they are doing." (Luke 23:34) If You can forgive those kinds of things and You were totally innocent, by Your strength and power, I can forgive the things that have been done to me. I also acknowledge the people who hurt me haven't always known what they are doing or what repercussions their actions would have.

Lord, You tell me to forgive others in the sight of Christ in order that Satan might not outwit me. Help me never to be unaware of his schemes. (2 Cor. 2:11) Please help me to see how much the enemy takes advantage of unforgiveness. I offer him a foothold any time I refuse to forgive.

THIS WEEK'S NUGGET:

LORD, I cry out to You; make haste to me! Give ear to my voice when I cry out to you. Let my prayer be set before You as incense, the lifting up of my hands as the evening sacrifice.

Psalm 141:1-2

TREASURES *of* DARKNESS

WEEK 2: THE TABERNACLE & PRAYER

- INTRODUCTION -

I began writing this week at the threshold of Psalm 141 - a psalm written by David while he was being pursued by Saul. As you read it, envision one man that God would make king, hiding in a cave from the crowned king who's kingdom was about to be ripped away from him. If you'd like the background of what was actually happening around the time David was in the cave, read 1 Samuel 24. Those ten verses of Psalm 141 suddenly come alive when read in the right context.

If you did read 1 Samuel 24, you also read vs. 5-6 and saw David's heart become troubled after secretly cutting off a corner of Saul's robe. From an outsider's perspective, the man had every right to cut off a piece of his robe, let alone defend himself from the man that sought so violently to kill him. But God has specifically told him to *not do anything*. And the only way God could have done that was if David was spending time in prayer.

David cutting of a piece of Saul's robe was not sin outrightly. But it was disobedience for him. Sometimes God says no to things that aren't necessarily sin. It's happened a handful of times in my own life. Like the time I got my nose pierced when I was 18 with an ex-boyfriend. Two years (and a baptism) later, I was working at a coffee shop that didn't allow piercings. One day after work, I was walking to the bathroom to put my nose ring back in and felt God whisper *"Why do you still have that?"* So I stood in front of the mirror and thought *"if this slips out of my fingers and goes down the drain, I'll know that was the LORD."* Not two seconds later, it literally slipped right out of my fingers and went straight down the drain. It was the last piece of the old Jane.

There was also the time I had a particularly sticky business scenario. I received a series of emails that left the door wide open for me to get trapped if I didn't tread carefully. So I stopped and quickly asked for discernment before replying. And I suddenly saw the scenario through different eyes. And I replied differently. What I wanted to do was proverbially cut off a piece of the writers' robes and hand it right back to them. And I might have if I wasn't in prayer, asking for discernment. The tricky part was following up the discerning wisdom with kindness. Sweet words, as David describes in Psalm 141:6, not words spoken through clenched teeth. The type of kindness that David used when he communicated with Saul after cutting off the corner of his robe. After being close enough to kill the man that was so desperately trying to kill him. David replied with kindness.

"David arose afterward, went out of the cave, and called out to Saul, saying, 'My lord the king!' And when Saul looked behind him, David stooped with his face to the earth, and bowed down. And David said to Saul: 'Why do you listen to the words of men who say, 'Indeed David seeks your harm?' Look, this day your eyes have seen that the LORD delivered you today into my hand in the cave, and someone urged me to kill you. But my eye spared you, and I said, 'I will not stretch

out my hand against my lord, for he is the LORD's anointed. Moreover, my father, see! Yes, see the corner of your robe in my hand! For in that I cut off the corner of your robe, and did not kill you, know and see that there is neither evil nor rebellion in my hand, and I have not sinned against you. Yet you hunt my life to take it. Let the LORD judge between you and me, and let the LORD avenge me on you. But my hand shall not be against you.'" (1 Samuel 24:8-12)

David spoke to Saul in "the gentlest and most respectful language in regard to the injustice of his conduct towards him."[1] We get a rare glimpse here of a scenario acted out (1 Samuel 24) side by side with the prayer surrounding the circumstance (Psalm 141). In the psalm, David literally asks the LORD to set a guard over his mouth and to keep watch over the door of his lips. And, as a result, he spoke to Saul with kindness.

The Hebrew word used for mouth there is *peh*. The root word has the sense of breathing, which points straight back to where we started in the introduction to week one - with our breathing taking on the cadence of His breathing.

"God made my lips to be a door to my words. Let grace keep that door that no word may be suffered to go out which may in any way tend to the dishonor of God or the hurt of others." (Matthew Henry) [1]

The moral of the story is the mouth is a door that needs a watchman (an office that God will fulfill) and regular oiling (a need the Spirit will cover).

We'll wrap this up with 2 Timothy 2:16-17 and let you get on to your homework for the week. *"But shun profane and idle babblings, for they will increase to more ungodliness. And their message will spread like cancer."*

I did what I usually do, and studied up on the original Greek language that was used. With the information I gathered, the same verse can also be read this way:

"Literally turn yourself around to avoid ungodly and unvirtuous discussions of vain and useless matters, for they will actually make progress and push you toward wickedness. And their message will spread like cancer, and gnaw at the bones like a disease by which any part of the body suffering from inflammation becomes so corrupted that, unless a remedy be seasonably applied, the evil continually spreads, attacks other parts and, at last, eats away the bones."

So I pray like David prayed. *Set a guard, O LORD, over my mouth; and keep watch over the door of my lips ... for my eyes are upon You.*

---

1 Charles Spurgeon, *The Treasury of David: Psalm One Hundred and Forty-One* (Hendrickson Publishers, 1990), 311.

TREASURES *of* DARKNESS

WEEK 2: THE TABERNACLE & PRAYER

- DAY 1 -

Read Psalm 141:1-2, and then write the verses in your journal.

Now that you know the background on this Psalm, we can dig a little deeper into the heart of it. You now know that David is praying fervently. In distress. In the midst of affliction. Likely hiding in a cave from those seeking to kill him upon sight. Times like those make for some intense prayers. The kind that cut right to the chase. I read a quote by John Trapp on verse 1, and it's just as applicable today as it was in the 1600s when he wrote the sentence:

"No distress or danger, how great soever, shall stifle my faith or stop my mouth, but it shall make me more earnest, and my prayers, like strong streams in narrow straits, shall bear down all before them."

It's interesting that we've been studying about our mouths and our words, and the impossibility of taming our tongue, and then John Trapp talks specifically about how no distress or danger shall stop his mouth. It's a very obvious reminder of praying without ceasing. I bet if we paid more attention in giving due diligence to our prayer lives, we wouldn't be quite as worried about our tongues because they're already occupied.

Read 1 Thessalonians 5:17.

"'Pray without intermission'; without allowing prayerless gaps to intervene between the times of prayer." (Jamieson, Fausset & Brown)

"The meaning is not that men should do nothing but pray, but that nothing else we do should hinder prayer in its proper season." (Matthew Henry).

It's important to note the tense of the word "pray": an imperative mood in the present tense. In laymen's terms, the imperative mood is not a suggestion. Rather, it's an absolute command requiring full obedience on the part of all hearers. No pressure...

Praying without ceasing changes the thought process of "I prayed this morning" to "I've already prayed. But I'm going to *keep* praying. I've already cried out to You. But I'm going to *keep* crying out to You." Continually. Over and over again. Sometimes that's just habitual prayer about daily things. And sometimes it's fervent prayer for very specific things. In David's case, he was praying fervently. Out of desperation.

Read James 5:16, paying particular attention to the second half of the verse, then look it up online. If you click on the parsing for "the effectual fervent", you will see the phrase is in present tense. Anytime a word or phrase is in present tense, it's indicating a continuous or habitual action that often reflects a lifestyle. To get the full impact of the meaning, you can safely insert the word "continually" in front of it.

With that information, fill in the blank to show how the verse could now read: *"... the effective, fervent, _____ prayer of a righteous man avails much."*

Look up James 5:16 on blueletterbible.org and write the definitions for the following words:
" effectual fervent": _____
_____
_____

The fervency in this case shows action. If you look at the other verses listed that use this same Greek word, you'll see that the word is translated over and over again as "work". Working miracles. Things being worked out in us. An active process that produces a result. The root word for *energeō* actually means active. It's not passive by any means. Neither should our prayers be.

"availeth": _____
_____
_____

Did you take note of the parsing? This is another word in present tense. Our continual, active, fervent prayers yield continually active results. And I think it's interesting to mention that James made a point to include the word "effective" in front of "fervent prayer". Because prayer is always effective. It might not always be answered. But it's *always* effective.

Go ahead and read the rest of this section in James, ending in verse 18. You'll see a picture of another godly man praying another fervent prayer that God answered very specifically.

Spend the rest of your time today in prayer. Start flexing those prayer muscles. Write them out if you have to. Remember... the more our mouths are engaged in prayer, the less they'll be engaged in other unvirtuous things. And I don't know about you, but I definitely need more of that!

TREASURES *of* DARKNESS

WEEK 2: THE TABERNACLE & PRAYER

- DAY 2 -

Sometimes with prayer, there's a fervent need that can't be ignored. That was what we studied yesterday. Now that it's out of the way, we can begin actually digging into the picture of prayer that God intended from the beginning by looking at the sacrifices and offerings He set in place in the Old Testatment.

First, read Psalm 141:1-2, and then write it in your journal. We'll be camping out on the first part of verse 2 for the next two days. Once you have it written down, turn to Exodus 30.

I've done an entire study on the tabernacle before, and it's not light. It's a ten-week study complete with filling in the blanks, drawing diagrams, writing cross-references, and understanding the picture God so specifically put together for His people. I won't make you draw diagrams. But I am going to give you a crash course on the Tabernacle.

In Exodus 30, we find ourselves standing in front of the Altar of Incense. Assuming you are a Levite, a particular tribe of Israel that was especially assigned the tasks connected with the Tabernacle, you are now inside of it - as far as you can get inside without being in the actual Holy of Holies. You've already chosen the male animal without defect for the sacrifice, presented the animal at the door of the tabernacle, laid hands on the animal as a picture of transferring your sin, slaughtered it, skinned it, and cut it into pieces. You've already sprinkled the blood on the side of the altar of burnt offerings, arranged the wood, laid out the pieces of the animal, and burned the offering. You've already disposed of the ashes, cleaned up the mess, changed your clothes, and put on your linen garments. And that was all just to get *inside* the tabernacle where you are now standing.

After all that, you washed at the bronze basin (which was only reserved for Moses, Aaron, and Aaron's sons) before entering the Holy Place. The seven candles on the golden lampstand were already burning because of the measures that have already been taken, and the table of showbread was already meticulously prepared. And now you're standing at the altar of incense. Behind it is the veil separating you from the Holy of Holies. Whew. That's a lot of holy hoops to jump through just to be able to communicate with God!

Read Exodus 30:1-10. Based on what you read, write a brief description of how the altar of incense was to look:

_____
_____
_____

I can just imagine the golden touches everywhere. Doesn't that just sound like exactly what happens to us when we pray? We approach God as boring old acacia wood. Full of slivers and dirt. And when we are placed in His presence, we become covered in His Spirit. Overlaid in pure gold. Imperfections hidden. I can't help but think of a wedding ring that's made of white gold. Over time, the gold wears off and it needs to be re-dipped to maintain it's "white" appearance. We need to be consistently in His presence. Daily. Praying without ceasing. After all, we are the bride of Christ. How often was Moses instructed to tend to the altar of incense, and who was to do it (verse 7)?

_____

Now, skip ahead to Exodus 30:34-35. What was the incense to be made out of?

_____
_____

Go onto blueletterbible.org and look up the word "stacte", making sure to read the Gesenius' Hebrew-Chaldee Lexicon and see if anything interesting pops out at you:

_____

Did you catch it? The altar of incense includes three very specific ingredients that were also brought to Jesus upon His birth by the magi (Matthew 2:11). The gold that the table was overlaid in, the stacte (which myrrh flows spontaneously from), and pure frankincense. I just love how specific and intentional God is to so many of the smallest details in Scripture!

Continue reading the rest of the chapter. There are a lot of very specific instructions going into not only the building of the tabernacle and the execution of the services within, but also simply preparing the incense. Rubbing and beating the spices, until they are literally dust before presenting it to God. But here's the catch: according to one commentary I read, the priests were required to have a *full pound* of the pulverised, beaten-as-dust spices for each day of the year! It wasn't just a sprinkling. I also have to point out that Jesus was bruised and beaten for our sins when He was presented as our pure sacrifice on the cross.

Prayer isn't just a quick and easy thing. It's work. When Aaron wasn't busy tending to the lamps in the morning and at twilight, he was likely thinking about what needed to be done to be able to tend to them.

Praying without ceasing.

Spend some time simply enjoying God's presence. Talk with Him. He's waiting for you with a table prepared.

TREASURES *of* DARKNESS

WEEK 2: THE TABERNACLE & PRAYER

- DAY 3 -

I sat down this morning with my prayer journal open, ready to spend some time in the presence of God, and I was keenly aware of (and thankful for) how easy He has made it for us. No messy sacrifices required. No linen garments. Just me, my Bible, my pajamas, and my favorite blanket. I did make a point to light a candle, since we are studying prayer as incense. And I immediately took note of one thing: as we pray, and our prayers rise up to heaven like the smoke coming off of a flame, we are also affected. Our hearts and stubborness can only resist the flame so long before they start softening and melting like wax with the heat and the fervency of the prayers. The result of a burning candle? A home filled with a beautiful fragrance.

Read 2 Corinthians 2:15 and write it in your journal. Then go to blueletterbible.org and look up the verse.

Click on "sweet savour". Which word in the second definition particularly pertains to this week's study? _____

One commentary I read said that we not only *"scatter the savor, but we are the sweet savor itself" (Jamieson, Fausset & Brown)*. God help me to be an effective representation of Your fragrance of grace!

Back to Psalm 141. Yesterday we studied all that went into the preparation of the priests even entering the tabernacle, as well as the preparation alone for the altar of incense. I read a quote by Charles Spurgeon that explains this perfectly:

"As incense is carefully prepared, kindled with holy fire, and devoutly presented unto God, so let my prayer be. We are not to look upon prayer as easy work requiring no thought, it needs to be 'set forth;' what is more, it must be set forth 'before the Lord,' by a sense of His presence and a holy reverence for His name: neither may we regard all supplication as certain of divine acceptance, it needs to be set forth before the Lord 'as incense,' concerning the offering of which there were rules to be observed, otherwise it would be rejected of God."

I was talking with a friend last week about faith. And how the New Testament speaks of praying in full assurance that what we ask of Him, that He will do. Read Mark 11:24 and write the verse here: _____
_____
_____

The lesson is fairly clear: nothing can stand before a confiding faith in God. Not even mountains (Mark 11:23.) This is a key point to remember that we might be able to pray boldly, and in full confidence of His coming answer. Yet I feel like most Christians today (myself included) have lost a reverence when it comes to approaching God in prayer. We often treat Him more like a genie granting wishes than a holy God sovereignly working out His plan for our lives. Yes, we need to pray in full assurance of the answer, knowing that He hears and acts on our behalf. But I think we also need to take into consideration the pattern that God originally set up in the tabernacle to represent prayer.

The priests had to go through dozens of steps before they arrived at the altar of incense (which we've already discussed). One misstep meant the sacrifices wouldn't be accepted, and the holiness of the people they represented depended upon an acceptable sacrifice. They not only followed each step as an act of faith, they also did them with a weight of reverence on their shoulders. I think this is a perfect example of what it means to fear the Lord: knowing that we come to a God so holy there isn't even a word for it; knowing that we couldn't even begin to think ourselves of being worthy in His presence; knowing that He holds our very breath in our hands... and yet coming in full assurance that we will be accepted into His presence.

We need to find a way back to reverence in our prayer lives.

Go back to Psalm 141:2 on blueletterbible.org and look up the definition for "be set forth". When you're studying the Old Testament, you always want to check the parsing of the particular word you're looking up (if it's provided), because it will tell you which stem to pay attention to (this isn't usually the case when you're studying Greek words). In this case, you want to look up the Niphal stem. Jump to the Niphal section within the definition, and write a few of the key words below:

_____

_____

Setting my prayers before God in this sense means to fit, to establish, to make firm. *"The Psalmist desires that his prayer should not be like that which is feeble, languishing, easily dissipated; but that it should be like that which is firm and secure." (Albert Barnes)*

I want to leave you with part of a commentary by John Owen:
"There is a fourfold resemblance between [incense and prayer]:
1. In that it was beaten and pounded before it was used. So doth acceptable prayer proceed from a broken and contrite heart. (Psalm 51:17)
2. It was of no use until fire was put under it, and that taken from the altar. Nor is that prayer of any virtue or efficacy which is not kindled by the fire from above, the Holy Spirit of God, which we have from our altar, Christ Jesus.
3. It naturally ascended upwards towards heaven, as all offerings in the Hebrew are called 'ascensions,' risings up. And this is the design of prayer, to ascend unto the throne of God: 'I will direct unto Thee, and will look up.' (Psalm 5:3, 4)
4. It yielded a sweet savour; which was one end of it in temple services, wherein there was so much burning of flesh and blood. So doth prayer yield a sweet savour unto God; a savour of rest, wherein He is well pleased.

Look up both of the verses that were mentioned in Owen's commentary. Pray through them. And light a candle that will remind you of how our prayers ought to look as you catch whiffs of it every once in awhile throughout the day. Tomorrow, we begin to look at the evening sacrifices.

TREASURES of DARKNESS

WEEK 2: THE TABERNACLE & PRAYER

- DAY 4 -

Read Psalm 141:2 and write it in your journal with some sort of emphasis on the second part of the verse.

Hold on to your seats. The last two days were a crash course in the taberncale. Today is a crash course in sacrifices and offerings. It's a lot of information, and I pray that it's not overwhelming to you - but rather gives you a better understanding of prayer.

Go to Exodus 29 and read verses 38-46. How many times a day were the offerings given? _____

Remember back to the description I gave of the steps the priests had to go through with sacrificing the animals? It's a lengthy, messy process. Just when they finished cleaning up, they likely only had an hour or two before it had to be done it all over again.

There was a period in college that I struggled through a particularly dark season of depression during the day and incessant nightmares at night. For a handful of months, I was spending time with the LORD three times a day. Morning, noon, and night. And that was just to get through my day in one piece. I can't imagine doing that now - although I think, if the circumstances warranted it, I'd find the time. It's convicting to think of the act of tithing in reference to our prayer time. If we gave ten percent of our day to the LORD, we would spend nearly two and a half hours in prayer!

This was a full time job for the priests. One they were created for. Born into. The entire population of Israel depended on their diligence with these sacrifices to be accepted by God. Oh the things we'd see God do in our lifetime if we approached our prayer lives with that same sense of urgency!

Look back at Exodus 29. We're actually approaching this week's study somewhat backwards since we began with the altar of incense, and we're now backing out to the entrance of the tabernacle and the sacrifices that must be made before the priest even gets to the altar of incense. But we're going in the order of Psalm 141. So on we go.

We're going to take a closer look at the grain and drink offerings, which are to be made with the evening sacrifice.

You'll see a description of both grain and drink offerings given in Exodus 29:40. Write them here:
grain offering: _____
drink offering: _____

The sacrifices always included bread and wine. And since we're talking food, add in the lamb meat from the burnt offering and you have yourself a meal. Matthew Henry puts it this way in his commentary: *"Our daily devotions must be looked upon as the most needful of our daily works and the most pleasant of our daily comforts. Whatever business we have, this must never be omitted, either morning or evening; prayer-time must be kept up as duly as meat-time. The daily sacrifices were as the daily meals in God's house, and therefore they were always attended with bread and wine. Those starve their own souls that keep not up a constant attendance on the throne of grace."*

That's a pretty powerful (and convicting) reminder! I can't go for three hours without eating, and yet sometimes I'll go for a week or two (or four) without sitting at the throne of grace. I don't know why it's so hard to understand how important it is to communicate with God daily. How easily we forget.

Back to Psalm 141:2 - *"Let my prayer be set before You as incense, the lifting up of my hands as the evening sacrifice."*

I imagine that David specifically mentions only the evening sacrifice because he was likely hiding out in the cave for the night. Possibly around the time the priests were preparing for their evening sacrifice. I haven't read anything to support that - it's just my own idea. But coming from a man still living under the Old Testament laws, keenly aware that he was unable to make the daily sacrifices on his own, he prayed a fervent prayer out of desperation. *"Lord, I know I don't have a blameless lamb to sacrifice. I know I'm nowhere near a priest. Or a tabernacle. Or even any sort of official altar from which You will accept an offering. But I'm desperate. And I'm tired. So please... all I can offer is these empty hands. And this desperate heart. Please...just this once...will you accept it instead of an evening sacrifice?"*

How's that for faith? LORD, give me a heart like David's.

And as for application? Maybe carve out *two* segments of time for God today.

TREASURES *of* DARKNESS

WEEK 2: THE TABERNACLE & PRAYER

- DAY 5 -

I very clearly remember the first time I ever raised my hands in worship. It was a Tuesday night and I was standing in a room full of 200 college students for a weekly study. I had just been newly baptized, and God was beginning to change my ideas of what worship looked like. Being raised in a Presbyterian church provided a more traditional approach to worship. And while I had seen people with hands raised while they worshipped before, I was never comfortable enough to do it. But that night? It was suddenly more uncomfortable to *not* raise my hands than it was to raise them.

There is a direct correlation between prayer and worship. Our prayer, a lot of times, *is* worship. The two cannot be separated.

Since we're walking down memory lane, I also remember the first time a light bulb went off in my head regarding prayer. Growing up, we always "said grace" at the dinner table - the same sing-song poem every single night. My sisters and I each took turns saying it. "God is great, God is good. Now I thank Him for my food..." Then, one evening in the summer of 2000, I found myself in a tent on a Tennessee field. My friend was praying. And she was talking to God just like she would talk to me. Normal. Unrehearsed. As a friend. That moment completely changed my prayer life forever.

Read Psalm 141:1-2, and write the verses for the last time this week in your journal.

We spent the last part of our time together yesterday discussing the fact that David was likely hiding in a cave without access to any of the items (or people) he would need for the necessary daily sacrifices. As New Testament believers, we no longer have need of those sacrificial laws. But I imagine that raising my hands to heaven in praise, and in prayer, is the same effect as the sweet smell of incense flowing up to heaven. To Him, it all "smells" the same.

I want to look at both of these verses in their entirety again, and take note of David's desperate fervency we began this week with. Charles Spurgeon makes a very interesting point in his commentary on the Psalm: (picking up in the middle of verse 1) *"'Give ear unto my voice, when I cry unto Thee.' See how a second time he talks of crying: prayer had become his frequent, yea, his constant exercise: twice in a few words he says 'I cry; I cry.' How he longs to be heard, and to be heard at once! There is a voice to the great Father in every cry, groan, and tear of His children: He can understand what they mean when they are quite unable to express it."*
One night in 2012, I was wide awake at 2:30 am. It had been nearly six weeks since Shawna's shocking cancer diagnosis, and God was keeping me up many nights in what I called the Night Watch. Wide awake. Heart burdened. And yet, strangely, without the words to pray. I had been thinking all day about prayer. Supplication. Intercession. The full of

tears type of prayer. The "I can't breathe" type of prayer.

The wordless type of prayer.

I had read these two quotes back to back in a devotional that afternoon:

*"Emergencies call for intense prayer. When the man becomes the prayer nothing can resist its touch. Elijah on Carmel, bowed on the ground, with his face between his knees, **that was prayer – the man himself.** No words are mentioned. Prayer can be too tense for words. The man's whole being was in touch with God, and was set with God against the powers of evil. They couldn't withstand such praying. There's more of this embodied praying needed." (The Bent-Knee Time)*

"Groanings which cannot be uttered are often prayers which cannot be refused." (C. H. Spurgeon, Step-By-Step Grace)

Go to Romans 8:26 on blueletterbible.org. This time, go to "tools" and click on the "commentaries" tab. Scroll all the way to the bottom of the list until you find the text commentaries by Jamieson, Fausset and Brown. Click on "Commentary on Romans 8". You don't need to read the commentary on the entire chapter, just scroll down until you find *"26, 27. Likewise the Spirit also,"* and read that section, paying extra attention to the last paragraph.

"But not in vain are these groanings. For the Spirit Himself is in them, giving to the emotions which He Himself has kindled the only language of which they are capable; so that though on our part they are the fruit of impotence to utter what we feel, they are at the same time the intercession of the Spirit in our behalf."

That was profound to me. Even better? Every single time Aaron or his sons entered the tabernacle and tended to the altar of incense, they were making intercession for the Israelites. They lived to intercede for the children of God.

Read Hebrews 7:25 and write the second part of the verse here:

_____

It is our duty to spend time lifting our hands in prayer, and spending time with God, because our Savior lives to intercede for us. He's *waiting* to intercede for us.

Go to biblegateway.com (note: that's a different website than blueletterbible.org) and look up the Amplified version of Isaiah 30:18. Write every single rich word in your journal, and spend the rest of your time praying through and thinking on it. He's waiting for you.

THIS WEEK'S NUGGET:

Do not let your adornment be merely outward - arranging the hair, wearing gold, or putting on fine apparel - rather let it be the hidden person of the heart, with the incorruptible beauty of a gentle and quiet spirit, which is very precious in the sight of God.

1 Peter 3:3-4

TREASURES *of* DARKNESS

WEEK 3: THE BEAUTY OF HOLINESS

- INTRODUCTION -

Welcome back to another week of our journey together! You've jumped into the deep end of studying scripture and you're still here with me. That's a good sign! Last week, I ended the introduction to our week on prayer with a look at 2 Timothy 2 and a reminder to literally turn yourself around to avoid ungodly and unvirtuous discussions of vain and useless matters. We studied about how we can busy our tongues in prayer and the beautiful significance of the tabernacle and altar of incense in both its representation of prayer and the symbolic representation of the Spirit covering us in pure gold as we approach God through prayer.

This week, we're going to flip one book over and begin in 1 Timothy 2. We meet up again with Paul in a letter written to Timothy, a young pastor and spiritual son to Paul. We'll pick up in the middle of the chapter when he's discussing men and women in the church. The verses start with prayer and end with beauty - the perfect segue to what I felt like God was prompting for this week: the beauty of holiness.

"I desire therefore that the men pray everywhere, lifting up holy hands, without wrath and doubting; in like manner also, that the women adorn themselves in modest apparel, with propriety and moderation, not with braided hair or gold or pearls or costly clothing, but which is proper for women professing godliness, with good works." (1 Timothy 2:8-10)

I have a love-hate relationship with the topic of beauty in the church. I've been on the receiving end of well-intentioned modesty talks. I've watched first hand as girlfriends grabbled their way through the pendulum swing of always being perfectly put together and not being put together at all. Desperately trying to find the balance and sometimes also seeking to appease the convictions of those around them. When I was in college, I hadn't yet learned the cardinal rule that a white bra beneath a white shirt practically glows in the dark. Unfortunately, I learned that lesson after standing up to make an announcement before an audience of two hundred students. I remember the outfit clearly. And I felt particularly pretty that day. The next day I was taken out to lunch. As baskets of chips came and went, and salsa bowls were refilled, the conversation slowly turned to the night before. And the importance of modesty and covering up. I was wearing jeans and a turtleneck that night. I couldn't have been *more* covered up. But once the embarassment faded, I had learned that modesty is, quite literally, layered.

The topic of beauty is a sensitive one for me. But it's also a necessary topic to study. To dig into in scripture to see what the Bible *really* says on the topic. To measure your own line in the sand and find your own conviction. And, most importantly, to love the people around you that have their lines drawn in different places without trying to move their line a little closer to yours.

So I began to dig, studying through 1 Timothy 2:9-10 phrase by phrase. Word by word. This is what I discovered, and how it could read instead:

...in like manner also, that the women put themselves in order and embellish themselves with honor, chastity, purity, and worship in modest and appropriate, yet becoming, apparel, with regard for others - not seeking to turn the eyes, mind, or attention of anyone toward you. But rather, turning them toward God.

When Josh and I were very newly dating, I'm embarassed to admit that I was frustrated with the lack of attention I was receiving. We were dating! It was a big deal! And I wanted everyone to know and celebrate with us! One evening during worship, I saw a picture of a dark room. A handful of our friends were standing with their backs to me, worshiping. As I slowly walked by each, I looked at their faces. Eyes locked upward. Tight on Jesus. Unaware of my presence. And then I got to Josh at the front of the room. Incidentally at the end of an aisle. I looked at his eyes locked tight on Jesus. Unaware of my presence. And I was bothered. So I stood closer.

And then a little closer.

And when I still hadn't garnered his attention, I began literally jumping up and down in front of him until finally, he looked. And I'll never forget the look I saw on his face. Disappointment. Disgust almost. But not in the "Jane, you are disgusting" kind of way. It was more simply because I had taken his eyes off of Jesus.

That's the picture that formed in my brain again as I read the definition of *propriety*, also translated *shamefacedness* in the KJV.

Josh and I attended a church for a short time that was markedly put together. Every Sunday was a fashion show of Anthropologie and Free People. The longer we went, the more I felt the pressure. To be put together. To garner the flattery of the other women. To turn their eyes toward me and the perfectly executed outfit I created that morning. *That's not how church should be approached.* I was readying myself in the mirror and not readying my heart to approach a holy God in worship.

It's so important to survey our hearts. What is my mindset as I'm getting ready for church in the morning? Or for a meeting at work? Or happy hour with girlfriends? What am I thinking about?

LORD, go before us this week. Let Your beauty be upon us. Cover us. Teach us how much beauty is intinsic to holiness. That we might seek to turn the faces of the people around us toward You and not ourselves. Thank You that You make beautiful things from dust. And You make everything beautiful in Your time. Thank You that there is a place for beauty in our relationship with You. Beauty and holiness are not mutually exclusive. Rather, they go hand in hand.

TREASURES *of* DARKNESS

WEEK 3: THE BEAUTY OF HOLINESS

- DAY 1 -

We've all heard the verses on beauty. We've heard the talks on modesty. If you're like me, you could probably give them in your sleep. I knew I wanted to study beauty this week. But I also knew I wanted to approach it differently. Rather than memorizing a handful of verses of how a woman of God ought to look, I would rather bask in the presence of a holy God and allow His presence to transform me into the woman He created me to be. I'd rather immerse myself in His holiness and watch as it becomes part of my daily life. Because if you spend enough time in the garden, you start to smell like the flowers.

Convictions change in subtle ways which, in turn, impact the habits that are so hard-wired in us.

This week came with a little bit more diffculty in terms of digging up the treasures of gold that He had waiting. It began with part of Psalm 93:5 jumping off the page at me. While I was unsure of where I was supposed to go next (but fully assured of where I was *not*), I looked back at Psalm 93, and read it from the beginning.

Go to Psalm 93 and read the first verse. Write it here: _____
_____
_____
_____

As I studied the Hebrew words for this verse, I found something that surprised me. The Hebrew word used for "clothed" is *labash*. With that in mind, look up each of the following verses first in your own Bible, and then on blueletterbible.org:

Judges 6:34
1 Chronicles 12:18
2 Chronicles 24:20

When you survey the Hebrew lexicon for each of those verses, which Hebrew word do you see throughout all three?
_____

Labash is connected with the expression by which the Spirit of God is said to *put on* anyone, i.e. to fill them. I've heard the term "filled by the Spirit" or "the Spirit came upon them". But somehow, to have the Spirit of God put on a person as a garment is so much more.... rich.

Going even further, what happened after the Spirit clothed Himself with Gideon (Judges 6:34), Amasai (1 Chron. 12:18), and Zechariah (2 Chron. 24:20)? _____

I can't help but see a trend starting to form with this study. Whenever the Spirit clothes Himself with a person, He is about to use their very *breath* for His holy purpose.

Go back to Psalm 93. According to verse 1, what is the LORD clothed with? _____

Look up the Hebrew word for "majesty" and write both the word and the definition here: _____
_____

Flip over to Psalm 104 and write verse 1 here: _____
_____
_____

Look up the Hebrew word for "majesty" in Psalm 104:1 and write both the word and the definition here: _____
_____
_____

I'm sure you noticed that the first rendition of "majesty" spoke more of the glory of God. This second version speaks more of the display of His glory. Since this week was written at Christmas time, think of *ge'uwth* as the overall beauty of the Christmas tree, and *hadar* as the beauty of one individual Christmas ornament.

Charles Spurgeon had an interesting point regarding Psalm 104:1 - that God Himself was not to be seen (He didn't even show Himself to Moses), but His works (which can also be called His garments) are full of beauty and can't be missed. He then said this: *"Garments both conceal and reveal a man."* [1]

I thought those words were incredibly profound, and apply specifically to what we will be studying this week. So chew on it for today and keep it in your back pocket. We'll be returning to it.

In the meantime, allow Him to clothe Himself with you today. Allow holiness to adorn your house. Before you set everything aside, spend some time meditating on His overwhelming holiness. God, may we be women that enhance Your holiness, and not detract from it.

---

[1] *Charles Spurgeon, The Treasury of David: Psalm One Hundred and Four (Hendrickson Publishers, 1990), 431.*

TREASURES *of* DARKNESS

WEEK 3: THE BEAUTY OF HOLINESS

- DAY 2 -

We'll begin our time together in the psalms once again - one of my favorite places. Open to Psalm 29, and write verse two here: _____

_____

_____

We find ourselves again in the Old Testament and the days of sacrifices, offerings, and tabernacle worship. Think back to the quick crash course we did on the tarbernacle last week - specifically the altar of incense overlaid in pure gold. The gold overlay wasn't something unique to the altar of incense alone. The entire tabernacle and all it's articles were either made of gold or overlaid in it. There is no other clearer picture of holiness than pure gold. And the tabernacle was covered in it. Throw in the candles from the altar of incense, and I can easily imagine the dramatic display of beauty from within the tented walls that only the eyes of the sons of Aaron could see.

That is the literal meaning of what David is referring to in verse two of this psalm. When he speaks of worshiping the LORD in the beauty of holiness, I imagine that this vision of the tabernacle is not far from his mind. But we don't go to churches overlaid in pure gold. And we certainly don't have to replace our clothes with holy linen garments at the door before entering a service on a Sunday morning. The architecture, clothing, ceremonies, and rituals that were once required to be accepted by God are no longer important. But holiness still is. In fact, it's imperative.

Look up Psalm 29:2 on blueletterbible.org and write down the Hebrew definition for "in the beauty" here: _____

_____

Did you notice the additional clause in Gesenius' Hebrew-Chaldee Lexicon? When David said "worship the LORD in the beauty of holiness," he was talking about ornaments or apparel worn at solemn festivals *(not priestly dresses, as some have supposed)*. He's talking about normal, every day clothes. Anyone - not just the priests - can worship God in the beauty of holiness.

I don't know about you, but I'd rather be more concerned about the holy robes I'm wrapping myself up in than the clothes I'm going to put on for the day. When David wrote these words, the sanctuary of the tabernacle was the beauty of holiness. After all, it was perfectly patterned after the heavenly sanctuary awaiting us some day. Today, there is a beauty that is still inherently connected to holiness. And it comes as a direct result of spending time in the presence of God.

Read Exodus 34:29.

Moses had just spent 40 solid days alone with God on Mount Sinai. While he was up there, he begged to see God's glory. You can read what happened in Exodus 33:19-23. I'd love to know what happened between the end of chapter 33 and the beginning of chapter 34. We're left hanging with God telling Moses what He was *going* to do. We read nothing of what actually happened. Some things are just so glorious and so personal that they can't be put into words.

All I know is that when Moses came off that mountain, his face shone. And he didn't even know it! The word "shone" literally means "to send out rays". He might not have noticed the heavenly glory still radiating on his face, but Aaron sure did. And I can only imagine the look on his face!

I noticed a trend some years ago that I think is an interesting one. I began seeing that the amount of compliments I received from friends tended to be indicative of the amount of time I was spending alone with the LORD. It might sound like a strange statement to make, but I think a hint of what Moses experienced still happens today. The more time we spend in solitude with God, the more radiant we are. We might not notice it. But other people do.

Because there is an intrinsic beauty in holiness.

We're going to end with 1 Peter 3:3-4. Write it here and pray through it today - we're going to look at it more in-depth tomorrow. And if I haven't already said it yet... thank you for taking this journey with me.

_____
_____
_____
_____
_____
_____
_____
_____
_____
_____
_____

TREASURES *of* DARKNESS

WEEK 3: THE BEAUTY OF HOLINESS

- DAY 3 -

Picking up right where we left off yesterday, go back to 1 Peter 3 and re-read verses three and four.

I love the way The Message interprets this section of scripture (beginning with verse one of chapter three):

"The same goes for you wives: Be good wives to your husbands, responsive to their needs. There are husbands who, indifferent as they are to any words about God, will be captivated by your life of holy beauty. What matters is not your outer appearance—the styling of your hair, the jewelry you wear, the cut of your clothes—but your inner disposition. Cultivate inner beauty, the gentle, gracious kind that God delights in. The holy women of old were beautiful before God that way, and were good, loyal wives to their husbands. Sarah, for instance, taking care of Abraham, would address him as "my dear husband." You'll be true daughters of Sarah if you do the same, unanxious and unintimidated."

Really, we could end our day right there and you could spend the rest of your time praying through every rich word. But you know I won't let you off the hook that easily.

I will say that I went ahead and looked up every single word in verse three and there are no hidden treasures. What you see is what you get. That's probably for a specific purpose - finding the balance between enjoying the femininity God created in us and the obsession with looking perfect is already hard enough. But there is one key word in the New King James (NKJV) version of the verse that I, for one, am so thankful for. What do you think it is? _____

Did you write down "merely"? Or did you look to see what I had said first? (That's what I would have done!) If that one word was taken out of verse three, the entire tone of the verse would have changed. It could have read "do not let your beauty be outward." Period. Instead, that one little four letter word was thrown into the mix. Because (thankfully) there is a place for adornment - in moderation, within your own personal convictions.

The catch is in verse four. Write it here: _____
_____
_____

We've got to put more emphasis on the adornment of our soul than the adornment of our self. When we're finding the balance, the scale needs to be heavier on the spiritual side.

My bible has a margin translation of incorruptible that says "imperishable". The King James Version (KJV) renders it as "that which is not corruptible". Look up the Greek word for that part of verse four and write the definition here: _____

I have a confession to make. In 2006, I worked at a makeup counter. As part of our skincare training, we had to know how to sell a $70 night time serum to a customer by demonstrating how amazing the product was. This was my speech:

"Every single day, your skin gets attacked by free radicals in the air. These free radicals are the leading cause of aging attacking our skin today. What's a free radical? Think about slicing an apple. If you don't eat the apple slice right away, it starts to turn brown. The same free radicals that make that apple turn brown are attacking the skin on our face right now and we don't even know it. While we sleep, our skin repairs itself as best it can. The serum aides in the overnight process, not only repairing past damage, but also providing a layer of protection against tomorrow's damage."

Some days, if we were really pushing the product, we would have apple slices on display. One slice with the serum applied. One without. The one without the serum quickly turned brown. The one that was covered in it was sealed and protected against the free radicals in the air that attacked the apple and turned it brown. It remained in tact for a much longer amount of time. *But it eventually turned brown.*

That's what I think of when I think of the word "corruptible". We can't waste our time and money worrying about the inevitable. We need to invest in the *incorruptible*, never wrinkling (or browning), unaged beauty of our spirit.

Which two attributes does an incorruptible spirit have? _____

The KJV translates "gentle" as "meek" - a word I've always had trouble understanding the meaning of. But I think this sentence sums it up pretty well: "The gentle person is not occupied with self at all."

Look up "quiet" on blueletterbible.org and write the definition here: _____

As for quiet, well... let's just say that's not one of my natural qualities. I find it interesting that quiet, in this case, also means tranquil. I can't help but thnk of the times that I've been caught up in some sort of dramatic event, or have felt wronged in some way. Those are certainly not times I'm tranquil. But those are also times where I *need* to be.

I love Jamieson, Fausset & Brown's commentary on this part of verse four: *"Meek and quiet--meek, not creating disturbances: quiet, bearing with tranquillity the disturbances caused by others. Meek in affections and feelings; quiet in words, countenance, and actions."*

Matthew Henry also puts it this way: *"Meekness and calmness of spirit are, in the sight of God, of great price-amiable in the sight of men, and precious in the sight of God."* I know from personal experience that calmness is certainly a trait Josh appreciates - when I actually display it. I don't know about you, but my brain is full of things that I feel are just beyond my reach. If I want to be anything remotely like a 1 Peter 3 woman, I've got some praying to do! So I'll leave you to it.

TREASURES *of* DARKNESS

WEEK 3: THE BEAUTY OF HOLINESS

- DAY 4 -

When I was in college, I had a battle with the mirror. And when I say that, I don't just mean the bathroom mirror, I mean any shiny surface through which I could see some semblance of my reflection. I was torn between the obsession of making sure I looked perfect at all times, yet hating what I saw looking back at me. I know the psychology behind it, and how I got there: years of dating an emotionally abusive boyfriend that tossed me aside for any new girl he met. (The same one with the nose piercing and the introduction to week two.) I wanted to look like them. Act like them. Talk like them. I wanted to *be* them Anyone but myself. Until I thoroughly hated everything about my appearance. If I had a rare moment of feeling pretty, I didn't want to go to bed that night. I was convinced I would never feel (or look) that way again. I could go into much more detail with this story, but the culmination happened when God went out of His way to dramatically get my attention.

I was leaving for the weekend with a friend to go who knows where. But, before I left, I had an especially difficult night spending hours wandering from one mirror to the other in my aparment as I packed. And the longer I looked, the more twisted my own reflection became. My mirror was Satan's playground. And he was having a heyday.

I had one full-length mirror on my bedroom wall, as well as a large mirror attached to the dresser. (Because it's normal to have two mirrors in one ten-foot room, right?) Rather than actually being nailed into the wall, the full length mirror was sandwiched in between four nails so tightly that it wasn't going anywhere anytime soon. Two on top. Two on bottom.

When I returned home from my weekend, I walked into my room to find the full length mirror mirror-side down on the carpeted floor. As I lifted it up, I saw it was shattered. When I looked at the wall, all four nails still remained firmly in their place.

The mirror had shattered after falling two feet onto *carpet*. And *only the nails remained*. I knew at that moment that God was doing an intervention.

I can't tell you how I came out of that - just like with any stronghold, God healed me through a lot of prayer. But I do remember the day, a couple years after Josh and I had been married, that I realized I hadn't worried about how I looked in quite awhile. Years even. I can't tell you the relief that comes with healing from strongholds we shouldn't be carrying in the first place.

Go to blueletterbible.org. Look up Proverbs 31:30 and write it here: _____
_____

The verse is translated this way in the NKJV: *"Charm is deceitful and beauty is passing, but a woman who fears the LORD, she shall be praised."*

The KJV translates "charm" as favour. Look up "favour" in the Hebrew Lexicon, and write the words you find here: _____

If you read further in Gesenius' Hebrew-Chaldee Lexicon you'll see that *chen* also means gracefulness or beauty.

Now we're about to see just how harsh Scripture is going get on the subject. Look up the word for "deceitful" and write the very first word you see here: _____

I'm not sure why it was such a shock to me to read that. Really, to deceive *does* mean to lie. But somehow hearing the word "deceitful" to me evokes a sort of innocent trickery. But it truly is an all out lie. And, if we're going to do a word-for-word translation here, it's safe to say that beauty is a liar. We see it every day on magazine covers. I know the ins and outs of photoshop. I know how easy it is to sculpt a model's legs to make them appear thinner. To create some version of themselves that's just not there.

Go back to blueletterbible.org and look up the word "vain" (translated "passing" in the NKJV). Write the definition here: _____

The representation of the breath in Scripture is used for anything transitory. Frail. Temporary. Our breath won't last forever. Rather than wasting my breath on vain things, what should I reserve it for?

Write the last part of Proverbs 31:30 here: _____

I'm not going to lie - I love beauty. Fashion. Makeup. Curling my hair. Painting my nails. But we have to find the balance in those things. We need to learn how to maintain our femininity while also spending just as much time (if not more) adorning our spiritual selves with holiness than we do getting ready for our day. So our adornment isn't merely outward.

I read an article this week that said this: *"if a woman's beauty and charm are the extent of her virtues, what happens when time and the trials of life take their toll? This woman does not depend on beauty and charm for her success. She recognizes her need for God."*[1]

Start the clock today. Make it a point to invest more time here with the LORD than you do in front of the mirror. LORD, may we radiate Your beauty today.

---

1   Grace Communion International, Proverbs 31: Portrait of a Godly Woman

TREASURES *of* DARKNESS

WEEK 3: THE BEAUTY OF HOLINESS

- DAY 5 -

This week was more difficult for me to write than the previous two. I'm not sure why that is - maybe because there's so many different directions that studying beauty can take you. Or maybe it's because of my own personal resistance to the verses that have been misinterpreted or used in a negative connotation in regards to beauty. Regardless, I was surprised to find myself slipping back into old patterns just a few months before. Spending increasing amounts of time in front of the mirror. Comparing myself to how I looked in group settings. Wondering if I was pretty enough or dressed up enough. In reality, I was fulfilling an expectation of who I believed I was perceived to be, as well as the expectations girls around me placed on themselvs.

Three years earlier, I was an advertising designer at the local newspaper. When I started, the sales reps began talking to me about designer bags and high-end fashion magazines. I didn't understand why until, after some time, I asked. Because of the way I carried myself (and my department store clearance handbag), the women at my new job had everything they thought they needed to know about me from their very first impression - likely made within the first seconds of meeting me.

Based on that understanding of how my first impression can come across, I sometimes get caught up in "playing the part" - and that's exactly what happened in that summer of 2011. One evening shortly after, I was sitting on the back porch with my Shawna and the ridiculousness of it all began to be very apparent. As we talked about what it means to lose your hair from cancer treatment, I began shrinking inside. Here I was caught up in whether or not I was pretty enough for a night out, when she was doing whatever she could to maintain the few hairs that remained on her head. To feel beautiful for her husband in their most intimate moments. To feel feminine. (Oh, how I long for those back porch conversations again!)

If I struggle with feeling beautiful now, in the prime of my life and with a full head of hair...how will I feel when the hair is gone, and I'm suddenly stripped of what it is that makes women...women?

Read Isaiah 40:6-8, and then write it here: _____
_____
_____

With the theme of this study beginning to take shape, one particular phrase leapt off the page at me. What do you think it is?
_____

Every single human thing, however good it may be, is temporary. Charles Spurgeon says this: "(Man) has a beauty and a comeliness even as the meadows have when they are yellow with the king-cups, but, alas, how short-lived! No sooner come than gone, a flash of loveliness and no more!" In due time, the breath of God will come like a wind and, with one simple puff, blow it all away like dandelions on a summer afternoon.

I decided that night, on Shawna's back porch, that enough was enough. It was time to get past the struggle that kept rearing its ugly head (pun intended) once and for all. It's imperative that I feel just as beautiful in my sweats, or in jeans and a tank top, as I do in a cocktail dress. Because I might wake up one day without a single hair on my head.

While Shawna worked through the natural struggles of being a woman who had all but lost her hair completely, she didn't realize she was more radiantly beautiful without it. She was like Moses having come down off the mountain that we looked at yesterday. She understood just how fragile life is. And she was spending extended time in the presence of God daily because she *had* to in order to survive another day with her faith intact.

I want to be a woman that has others recognizing my radiance for the LORD first and anything else second. Because soon, my time will come. And the breath of God will blow on me. And when that happens, I want my legacy to be that I was a woman who *feared God*, and not that I had great hair. Or a closet to die for. Or the latest pair of Jimmy Choos.

Read Psalm 90:17 and write it here: _____
_____
_____

This has become one of my very favorite verses, and I pray it regularly. I have for years. Over my life. Over my marriage. Over my creativity and my business. Make it your prayer today as we wrap up this week:

*God, let **Your** beauty be upon me. Not what I perceive beauty to be. Not the result of spending an hour doing my hair. But **Your** beauty. Let Your holiness adorn me more than the clothing and jewelry and makeup that I adorn myself with. Make me into a woman of grace, with a meek and tranquil spirit. Let Your holiness and Your beauty be enough for me, God. The beauty of You is the beauty of holiness, "that beauty in which the Lord Jesus Himself shone with lustre so resplendent, and which ought to be repeated or reflected by every disciple." Reflect Yourself in me today, according to Your grace. Let **Your** beauty be upon me.*

THIS WEEK'S NUGGET:

*An excellent wife is the crown of her husband,
but she who causes shame is like rottenness in his bones.*

Proverbs 12:4

TREASURES *of* DARKNESS

WEEK 4: CROWNING GLORY

- INTRODUCTION -

We talked last week about beauty. And holiness. And we discovered that although there is plenty of empty beauty without holiness, you will never find holiness without beauty. We put a magnifying glass over 1 Peter 3:3-4, looking in-depth at what the Bible has to say on the topic of beauty. We're going to spend our time this week in that same chapter. Two verses earlier. This week, we're going to study marriage.

Before we go any further, I want to stop here for a moment. There is need of recognition. For the single women. The separated or divorced women. The widows. There are plenty of women reading these words right here, right now, who experience a piercing sorrow in their heart at the word "wife". You might be tempted to skip over this week, but there is one promise tucked away in the Old Testament that might give you some incentive to keep reading.

"For your Maker is your husband, the LORD of Hosts is His name." (Isaiah 45:5)

As I was preparing to teach this week to a small group of women, I was keenly aware of a woman in the group that was in the process of getting a divorce. My heart was heavy for her, knowing this week would be a difficult one. As I was digging for the verse above with plans forming to teach on how He is our Husband first and foremost, I was also listening to a new live worship album. The woman leading worship was encouraging those in attendance to sing out in the Spirit. To lift their voices. "Every woman. *Every mother.* Lift your voice tonight," she said. I'm pretty sure I rolled my eyes and skipped to the next song. Because I was immediately excluded.

I'm not a mother.

And then I found that Maker-is-your-Husband-verse I was looking for in Isaiah 45:5. And I backed up to the beginning of the chapter to read it in context. And I stopped in my wallowing tracks.

*"'**Sing o barren**, you who have not borne! Break forth into singing and cry aloud, you who have not labored with child! For more are the children of the desolate than the children of the married women,' says the LORD." (Isaiah 54:1)*

At the very same moment I wanted to slink away and sulk, God was pulling me back. *Don't leave just yet. I've got something for you.*

The worship continued. *You turn my mourning into joy. My mourning into joy.* Oh LORD may I never leave your presence because I feel excluded.

I was preparing to teach on how an excellent wife is the crowning joy of her husband. And in that moment, I began to think about what it looks like to be a crowning joy to the LORD. He took my sin. The crown of thorns pressed into His holy head. *LORD help me to be the **jewel** in Your crown and not a thorn.*

In Psalm 17. David asks God to keep him as the apple of His eye - a term indicating that something or someone is cherished above all others. When Josh and I got married, we wrote our own vows. It was so important to me to replace the words *"I take you as my husband"* with *"**I choose you** above all others"*. I wanted to be chosen - not taken.

David is asking to be kept as the apple of God's eye. To be cherished. Exclusively. As if he were the only one on the planet. Because the hard-to-believe reality is if you were the only person on the planet, He still would have died for you. He still would have chosen *you*. Even when our marriages are faulty and our husbands disappoint, **He does not.**

The first references to that phrase David uses are actually Biblical: Psalm 17:8, Deuteronomy 32:10, Proverbs 7:2, Lamentations 2:18, Zechariah 2:8. It all started with a supernatural picture of His love for us. The literal translation is *Little Man of the Eye*, a reference to the tiny reflection of yourself that you can see in other people's pupils if you look closely enough. As a photographer, I always look for myself in the pupils. It's how I measure if a photograph is truly in focus or not. And the only way you can see yourself is if you're staring straight into the eyes of another person. *LORD lock my eyes tight on you.*

If (according to Isaiah 54:1) I'm raising spiritual children, then it makes sense that He is my Husband.

Hang on tight. We're about to become jewels.

TREASURES *of* DARKNESS

WEEK 4: CROWNING GLORY

- DAY 1 -

Every Sunday night for the last four weeks, I've sat down with my Bible and prayer journal open and actively sought God for what He has for the next week's homework. This week, just like every other week, He's laid it all out very clearly. Just like weeks past, I write this homework for day one not knowing how day five will end. To be honest, I don't even know how day two will begin. That's the most exciting part of this journey for me - watching God reveal Himself over and over again. I even wrote in my journal tonight that it's so astounding, it makes me want to laugh and cry all at the same time. All I know is I'm on to His trail for this week. And I can't wait to see what He has along the way for us.

Read Proverbs 12:4 and then write it here: _____

_____

In addition to being an avid journaler, I love to write in the margins of my Bible. In my Bible, the word "crown" is at the end of a line. At some point in time (who knows when), I changed "crown" to read "crown(ing joy)". It's not grammatically correct, but when I read the verse now, it says:

"An excellent wife is the crown*(ing joy)* of her husband..."

I don't know about you, but I want nothing more than to be the crowning joy of my husband. However, even though I've read and re-read the definition of virtue, I still find myself stumped as to what, exactly, a virtuous woman looks like.

Matthew Henry has a handful of definitions that fall under his commentary of what a virtuous woman is, based on Proverbs 31. Read the list below and check off the characteristics that you believe pertain to you:

_____ She is pious (showing devotion for deity and devotion to divine worship; the opposite of secular).
_____ She is prudent (shrewd, cautious, sensible).
_____ She is active for the good of her family. (Are you *actively* seeking things that are to the benefit of your family or, if you are without children, both you *and* your husband? Or do you make decisions based on how it best benefits you?)
_____ She looks well to the ways of her household (a reference to Proverbs 31:27 - in other words, do you wisely manage the things under your control within your household - cleaning, laundry, grocery shopping, etc.).
_____ She makes conscience of her duty in every relation. (Are you aware of what's expected of you?)
_____ She is a woman of spirit.
_____ She bears crosses without disturbance.

Let me just interject for a moment and speak specifically about item #4 in that list. Just this afternoon, I was thinking about the idea of household chores. Specifically: why is the wife the one that is expected to do all the "household" things? (Yes, my thought was in *that* tone.) And then I read verses like Proverbs 31:27. And 1 Timothy 5:14. Darn it. When it's there in black and white in Scripture, I can't argue with it - I simply have to pray that I will be better about it.

Just for good measure, read 1 Timothy 5:14, and then write it here: _____
_____

And since we're on the topic, I have a note about item #8 in that list as well. Josh's grandpa, who we affectionately call "Grampy" has been living with a constant migraine. And by that I mean, one solid migraine headache. Without relief. For well over a decade. But you'd never know it unless... well... you knew it.

Grampy is the most kind, loving, gentle man you could ever meet. And you'd only know of his never-ending migraine if he told you about it. I can't say I'd have that much grace and dignity if I had to bear that cross. In fact, I complain if I have a hang nail.

I can admit in full honesty and humility that I was only able to check off just a handful of things from that list. But I have a whole fistful of things to pray about.

I want to leave you with this quote by Elizabeth George from her book *Beautiful in God's Eyes*:

"God's beautiful woman is pleased to be her husband's crown. Shunning the spotlight, she gladly gives her life behind the scenes so that her husband may be noticed and honored. She is glad when he is the center of attention, when he excels, when he is recognized, when he rises to the top. Indeed, she delights in living in his shadow. His promotion is her greatest reward. She desires that her husband be highly respected and esteemed, so she contentedly offers the supreme sacrifice of herself for him."

*God, I pray that You would make me to be a woman who is not only pleased to be her husband's crown, but is also, without a doubt, her husband's crowning joy. Teach me how to be the wife **he** needs me to be - not just the wife I think I'm capable of being. Bring me beyond what I think I am capable of to meet the needs he doesn't even realize he has. Make me my husband's crowning glory. And through it, glorify Yourself.*

Spend the rest of your time in your journal. Pray specifically over the items on the previous page that weren't checked off. Ask Him to build those characteristics in you. Because we all need some spiritual intervention to love our husbands better. Deeper. Truer. More respectfully. The way they need to be loved.

TREASURES *of* DARKNESS

WEEK 4: CROWNING GLORY

- DAY 2 -

If you're like me, you're still chewing on that list we went through yesterday. I'm especially convicted about the qualities I wasn't able to put a check mark next to, and spent some time this morning praying that God would teach me how to find those habits. The harsh reality is that we're never going to be the perfect wife. But we can certainly do our best to pray about and exercise the qualities we lack. In doing that, both our husbands, and God, are blessed.

Go back to Proverbs 12:4 - we're going to look at the not-so-pretty second part of the verse. Write it here:
_____

As always, we're going to begin by looking up the Hebrew words. Start with "she that maketh ashamed":
_____

Did you make note of the tense before you started? And while you did that, you should have noticed the "participle" aspect. If you think back to week two, we discussed the importance of when the present tense is used in the New Testament. Anytime you see a word or phrase in the present tense, you can safely insert the word "continually" before it. The "participle" aspect of a Hebrew word indicates the exact same thing. It represents an action or condition in its unbroken continuity. In this context, it is a woman ontinually shaming her husband (and it's not the shamefacedness we discussed in the introduction to last week's homework). Continually nagging. Wearing down. Pushing buttons.

I hope you aren't surprised to know that Matthew Henry also has a list of qualities found in the wife who causes her husband shame. I grimace even as I write this:

_____ She is silly. (Exhibiting or indicative of a lack of common sense or sound in judgement; naive; 2 Timothy 3:6 references a "silly woman" or, in the NKJV, a "gullible woman". It's also translated "spiritually dwarfed".)

_____ She is slothful (sluggish, lazy).

_____ She is wanton (Isaiah 3:16 describes the wanton woman - making eyes and looking around for a new man; to feel the impulse of sexual desire for a man who is not your husband).

_____ She is wasteful and wanton (wanton is listed twice because there are two different definitions for the word - the second being wanton for things; wasteful with what you have yet wanting still more - James 5:5 KJV).

_____ She is passionate and ill-tongued. (Everything we spent our first week studying - Proverbs 4:24; but not just speaking about the tongue in general. This is specifically referring to how you speak when you're passionate about something. When you're worked up. When you feel wronged.)

_____ She ruins both the credit and comfort of her husband. (She has affected the honor and respect given to her husband, both in public and at home.)

Hello conviction - I think I'm ready to just shrink away and pray now. Just like yesterday, I do have one note I want to expand on: Because a husband and wife come in a unit package, the impression of one will always be applied to both. Far be it from me that I affect my husband's reputation because of my own impulsive and selfish actions, words, and habits!

Go back to Proverbs 12:4, and look at the very last part of the verse.

According to the Hebrew lexicon, what does "rottenness" mean: _____

A shameful wife is literally the spiritual decay of her husband. Many other translations render "rottenness" as "cancer". And when I begin to think of the side effects of cancer, it's even more important to avoid that list like the plague! I've seen firsthand the peeling skin. The hair loss. The diminished appetite and sensitivity to smells. The nausea and diarrhea. The inability to do any of your "cheer me up" list of favorite things because those side effects affect every single item on the list.

Every negative decision I make, every gossip-ridden or anger-filled conversation I choose to have, and every knee-jerk reaction I indulge directly affects my husband. It wearies him. It literally saps his strength until there's nothing left. And, sadly, there's not much he can do about the scenario unless I decide I want to change it.

Cancer is aggressively treated with chemotherapy that poisons the cancerous cells. We have to be just as proactive in treating the tendencies and characteristics we see in ourselves in the list on the previous page. Scripture and prayer are poison to sin. It's the only way to kill those habits.

I'll leave you with this quote on Proverbs 12:4 by Henry. Tomorrow we'll begin looking at the dreaded "s" word - submission. In the meantime, I believe we have a lot to pray about.

"A virtuous woman...is submissive and faithful to [her husband] and by her example teaches his children and servants to be so too. He that is plagued with a bad wife is as miserable as if he were upon the dunghill; for she is no better than rottenness in his bones, an incurable disease, besides that she makes him ashamed. If he go abroad, his head is hung down, for his wife's faults turn to his reproach. If he retire into himself, his heart is sunk; he is continually uneasy; it is an affliction that preys much upon the spirits."

*God, teach me how to be an excellent, virtuous wife. I'd much rather be the crown on his head than cancer in his bones. Show me the habits, qualities, and tendencies that I need to attack with prayer and scripture. Open my eyes to the things I might not be aware of. Help me to not defend those things and compare his negative qualities against mine. Let me simply seek change for **Your** glory. Because without You, I'll never win this fight.*

TREASURES *of* DARKNESS

WEEK 4: CROWNING GLORY

- DAY 3 -

I sat down this morning thinking about our study last week - specifically the verses we looked at in the Old Testament where God came upon Amasai, Gideon, and Zechariah. The part where God wraps Himself with us. The only way I will be able to put off the shameful characteristics we studied yesterday, and put on the prized characteristics we studied in day one is by His Spirit. Lord, fill me with Your Spirit and enable me to be the wife You've called me to be!

Go to 1 Peter 3. We spent some time studying verses three and four last week. This week, we're going to look at verses one and two. Read them in your Bible, and then write the verses here: _____
_____
_____

This chapter picks up where the previous one left off: with submission. Chapter two speaks of how servants should submit to their masters, and chapter three carries on the conversation talking about wives and marriage. I know - it's a controversial topic. But it doesn't have to be.

So many people get the impression that the idea of submission is a negative one. One of abuse. Instead, it's a matter of respect. Our husbands are an authority in our lives. They have a great deal of influence on us, and were created to be in the leadership position. We need to respect them enough to let them.

Go to blueletterbible.org and look up 1 Peter 3:1-2. We're going to look at the word "submissive" today but, before you do anything else, look at the tense of "[be] in subjection". Based on what we've learned about this particular tense, fill in the missing word that we know can be applied to this verse:

"Wives, likewise, be _____ submissive to your own husbands..." (NKJV)

Now look up the Greek lexicon for "[be] in subjection" Write a few of the definitions that stand out to you.
_____
_____

I loved the extra definition in the grey box: *"this word was a Greek military term meaning 'to arrange [troop divisions] in a military fashion under the command of a leader'. In non-military use, it was 'a voluntary attitude of giving in, cooperating, assuming responsibility, and carrying a burden'".*

Now flip over to Genesis 2:18.

The Hebrew word for "helper" or what the KJV translates as "help meet" is *'ezer*. There are no hidden nuggets in this definition - in this particular case, what you see is what you get. To help. To succour.

I'll be honest - I had to look up what "succour" meant. To succour is to provide assistance in time of difficulty or be an ally in war. By nature, an assistant is in a subordinate position contributing to the fulfillment of a need. What a clear picture of what the role of a wife looks like. Shows like Survivor have made the word "alliance" a common phrase. To ally yourself with someone is to form a connection. Or, more literally, to *bind* yourself to them.

Skip down a few verses and read Genesis 2:24. The idea of a husband and wife being joined is speaking of an especially firm joining. One of glue. If I glue two pieces of paper together, there is always one side that's up and one side that's down. This might be an overly simplistic example, but God created marriage so that the husband is on the front side of the paper, and the wife is on the back. He's forging into the storm, and we're covering his back as his rear guard.

Read Isaiah 52:12 and write the verse here: _____
_____

Our culture has twisted the idea of submission into a negative one. I believe wives are called to be our husband's rear guard. If, according to this verse, the LORD is leading from the front, and the God of Israel is also simultaneously protecting from the back, that can't be a bad role. In fact, it's just as important.

So often we waste our time trying to flip the paper so that we can be the one forging the way that we leave our husbands exposed and vulnerable for spiritual attack. It's his duty to make the decisions and trust what he feels like God is telling him. It's ours to provide the spiritual assistance. To pray. To support. To encourage. And to submit. Because if I'm busy pulling in the opposite direction that he wants to go, all my resistance will do is tear us apart.

God help me to let go of any preconceived notions of what submission looks like. Show me specific areas in my life today where I'm resisting submitting to my husband. Then, I pray for the strength to be able to let go of my own control and trust Your leading through him. Forgive me for ways that I've been disrespectful when I don't agree with a decision he has made. I need Your Spirit, God, to be content in the role You've asked me to fulfill.

If God is laying specific things on your heart today, write them down in your journal. Pray through them. Apologize to your husband in full humility and sincerity if you need to - *without expectation of reciprocation*. Stop resisting. Stop fighting. Simply cleave to him. Adhere yourself to him. Especially firmly, as if with glue. *Just cling.*

TREASURES *of* DARKNESS

WEEK 4: CROWNING GLORY

- DAY 4 -

We're going to pick up right where we left off yesterday, and continue studying 1 Peter 3:1-2. Write both verses again here, making sure to throw in the present active participle reference for good measure: _____
_____
_____

I just love reading the Amplified version of the Bible in my quiet time. It attempts to take both word meaning and context into account in order to accurately translate the original text from one language into another, providing us with a deeper understanding of scripture without having to do the digging ourselves. The Amplified version of 1 Peter 3:1 says this: *"In like manner, you married women, be submissive to your own husbands [subordinate yourselves as being secondary to and dependent on them, and adapt yourselves to them], so that even if any do not obey the Word [of God], they may be won over not by discussion but by the [godly] lives of their wives..."*

What practical definitions of submission to pray through and to strive for!
- God, help me to be secondary to my husband, putting him first in our marriage and in the decision making.
- LORD, teach me how to depend on him for all my needs - physically, emotionally, and spiritually.
- God, give me the strength to adapt myself to him, and not force him to change for me.

"... so that even if they don't know Christ, they will be won over *by the conduct of their wives.*" *Not by discussion.* Oh boy, another point of conviction. Sometimes it's better to just shut our mouths and pray (letting God display Himself through us whether or not we realize it) than to keep talking, further irritating our husbands to prove a point.

When Josh and I first got married, I was newly graduated from college with a fresh degree in photography and I was ready to use it. Four months later, we moved to Bend, Oregon, and I got a job at Starbucks. Then I was a marketing assistant and graphic designer at a home-building company. And then a makeup artist. And then an advertising designer at the newspaper. I was ready to pursue my dream...but Josh didn't think it was time yet. So I waited. *For three years.*

When I finally started my business, I also maintained two full time jobs on top of it. And I kept the pace for two years because Josh didn't feel peace about me quitting and pursuing a business that may or may not work. It was a risk he wasn't ready to take and I understood that. At one point, I was working fifteen hour days to be able to pursue my dream. Then the day came, two months shy of the third year anniversary of starting my business, when I finally received the green light from him to quit my job. That was in 2010, and I haven't looked back since.

I've learned over the years, that Josh feels the most respected if I wait when he asks me to wait. That span of five years of waiting to pursue my dream was difficult but, more than anything, it taught me how to wait on the LORD for His timing and provision. It also taught me the amazing blessing of doing things in God's timing. I now have an incredible business that is established as a result of the time frame God gave to Josh and not to me. And Josh was honored and respected because I yielded to his advice.

We're going to finish our time this morning looking at the second verse of 1 Peter 3. I want to begin by sharing the verse with you from the Amplified version - an interpretation I loved so much that I made it part of my vows when Josh and I got married. It's an exhaustive, all-inclusive picture of how the conduct of a godly wife should look: *"...they may be won over not by discussion but by the [godly] lives of their wives, when they observe the pure and modest way in which you conduct yourselves, together with your reverence [for your husband; you are to feel for him all that reverence includes: to respect, defer to, revere him--to honor, esteem, appreciate, prize, and, in the human sense, to adore him, that is, to admire, praise, be devoted to, deeply love, and enjoy your husband]."*

Our husbands won't be swayed by a heated argument, or a well-thought out point that suddenly proves them wrong. Instead, they will feel attacked and disrespected. They will be won over by our genuine love for Christ, that's naturally carried out through our deep respect and reverential fear for them.

Write down each description of what it looks like to show reverence for your husband:

1. _____
2. _____
3. _____
4. _____
5. _____
6. _____
7. _____
8. _____
9. _____
10. _____
11. _____
12. _____
13. _____

I believe we have quite a bit to pray through this week. Maybe we pray through each of these characteristics for the next 13 days, asking God to transform us in ways that we *need* to be transformed. One last thing before we go: find some time today to ask your husband what is the one thing you do that causes him to feel the most respected. Write it here:

_____

Then ask what is the one thing that causes him to feel the most disrespected - but here's the key: when he answers *do not* defend yourself, or answer back. Simply apologize, and start praying.

TREASURES *of* DARKNESS

WEEK 4: CROWNING GLORY

- DAY 5 -

We're going to end our time this week looking at two verses that serve as bookends for Paul's section on marriage in his letter to the Ephesian church. Thankfully, a good chunk of that is addressed to husbands (they need some instruction too, sometimes!) so we won't be studying it in its entirety.

Read Ephesians 5:22, and write the verse here: _____
_____

I love how The Message interprets this section of Ephesians, lumping verses 22-24 together: *"Wives, understand and support your husbands in ways that show your support for Christ. The husband provides leadership to his wife the way Christ does to his church, not by domineering but by cherishing. So just as the church submits to Christ as he exercises such leadership, wives should likewise submit to their husbands."*

We won't be looking up the words for this verse because the same Greek words are used here that we looked up a couple of days ago. But I do want to include the Amplified version of the verse here: *"Wives, be subject (be submissive and adapt yourselves) to your own husbands as [a service] to the Lord."*

What is an example of a way you've adapted yourself to your husband, even though it wasn't easy?
_____
_____
_____
_____

When I yield to my husband, I'm actually submitting to the LORD - honoring Him first and Josh second. Somehow this makes submitting easier, especially if I don't agree with the decision. I have to tell myself that it's coming from the LORD - whether or not it's the choice He would have wanted Josh to make, God is more honored in my submission to my husband than He ever would be in my resistance.

A woman that I knew through the church I attended in college was speaking at a women's retreat around 2001. During the first session, she shared her testimony. I'll condense her hour-long message as best I can while still allowing you to understand the full impact. Teri shared about her lifelong struggle with severe clinical depression. I don't just mean "I'm a little sad today" - I mean she couldn't get out of bed. For weeks. She was debilitated and unable to care for herself, let alone her children. Her five year old daughter was bringing her meals in bed. She'd tried countless medications, but nothing managed to clear the darkness that surrounded her mind.

Then, one day, her doctor suggested one more medication, convinced it would work. Her husband, however, was fed up with the constant stream of medications, new side effects, hope and expectations, and disappointment. To Teri, this medication was her last chance. Without it, she was of the absolute conviction that she was facing a death sentence. But her husband stood his ground. He did not want her to take it. And then she said these words that I will never forget:

"I didn't take it. Even though I knew it was a death sentence for me, I would rather die and go to heaven submitting to my husband than living in disobedience to him and to God."

The result? She submitted to her husband. God changed his heart. And the medication changed both their lives.

Skip down a few verses in Ephesians, read the last part of verse 33, and write it here: _____
_____

My Bible uses the word "respects". If you look up that work in the KJV, it's translated as "reverence" which also means "fear". But if you dig around in the Thayer's Lexicon, you'll see the word expounded upon further: "to reverence, venerate, to treat with deference, or reverential obedience."

The Amplified version explains it this way: *"Let the wife see that she respects and reverences her husband [that she notices him, regards him, honors him, prefers him, venerates, and esteems him; and that she defers to him, praises him, and loves and admires him exceedingly]."*

Another amazing, rich, and somewhat daunting prayer list. Take some time in your journal and turn each and every one of those things into a very specific prayer. It's amazing how your heart begins to swell with love for your husband when you pray to become the wife he needs you to be and not trying to change him into the husband you want him to be.

THIS WEEK'S NUGGET:

*I have learned in whatever state I am.
to be content.*

Philippians 4:11

TREASURES of DARKNESS

WEEK 5: CONTENTMENT

- INTRODUCTION -

This week's introduction came to me as a part two to what is actually next week's introduction: a study on the bones of character. And a promise that we will not be crushed under any affliction. But I won't spoil the ending. Instead, I'll share with you as it is written in my journal. As He gave it to me. Just as this entire study has been written so far.

(8:45am) Wednesday, 12/21/11

"Every burden you are called upon to lift hides within itself a miraculous secret of strength." (J.R. Miller)

Two days ago, I was studying the bones of character. LORD, I know I'm supposed to continue down this same path. Specifically, Ezekial 37. I pray You would illuminate my understanding with Your Spirit this morning.

Ezekiel 37:1 greets us with the hand of the LORD bringing Ezekiel, a prophet, into the middle of a valley full of bones. Very dry bones. Scattered about. Tossed aside. Discarded. Given up. And He asks Ezekiel four simple words: "can these bones live?" Next week, we will learn the bones of character - faith, hope, and joy. But this week, we can simply replace those with the bones. Can faith live? Can hope survive? Can joy breathe another day in our being?

Can I still find hope that's been set aside? Hope that's been lost? Can it be revived?

I shook my head when I saw the cross-reference: 1 Samuel 2:6. A story so familiar to me. But I've always lingered in chapter one. Finding strength in Hannah's found strength. I haven't paid much attention to chapter two, which is where Ezekiel takes me: to the song that came from Hannah's answered prayer. After she very nearly lost her faith altogether.

In 1 Samuel 1, Hannah is at her wit's end. Weeping. Not eating. Likely not sleeping.

This is not a woman whose faith is strong and whose hope is sure at the moment. And adding to her pain: her husband's second wife continually provoking her, and a husband that can't begin to understand the emotional turmoil of having a closed womb in a day when infertility was a reproach.

She was in bitterness of soul. And she wept in anguish. Praying fervently. And the priest thought she was intoxicated because of her inconsolable display of emotion.

There is something to be said for pure, raw, honest approaches to the throne of grace. Hannah put it all out there at the *door of the tabernacle (as close as she could possibly get to the presence of God) as she had done **so many** times before. And she allowed the God of all comfort...to **be** her comfort. Then she went her way and ate, and her face was no longer sad. And then she conceived. And God gave her a miracle baby. And she fulfilled her vow to God - giving her son that she had prayed so many years for back to Him.*

I don't think the timing was accidental. And it might be that the prayer of anguish she said in such raw emotion in verse 11 of chapter one was unlike any other prayer she had prayed before. So I need to stop and ask myself:

Why do I want children?
- *Simply because it's the next step in marriage?*
- *Because all my friends have them and I feel like a fish out of water without them?*
- *Because I feel like somehow I deserve them and have been robbed of a blessing all these years?*

Or is it because I want to see God glorify Himself? *Once my prayer is answered, will I simply be on my way? Or will I give that child back to the LORD freely and openly, for the rest of their life and mine?*

Hannah had come to the end of herself. God breathed new life into her faith. She was no longer crying. No longer discontent. No longer in want of something she didn't have but craved so deeply. Her appetite was back and she was no longer sad. In fact, she probably glowed. And then she sang.

Verse six of chapter two provides the cross reference back to Ezekiel 37: "The LORD kills and makes alive; He brings down to the grave and brings up."

There is no chance or fate in anything. Everything is dictated by the absolute sovereignty of God.

And so I pray like David prayed (one of the best ways to pray) in Psalm 51:8 - make me to hear joy and gladness today, LORD. Show me how, in the midst of my want, to be content.

TREASURES *of* DARKNESS

WEEK 5: CONTENTMENT

- DAY 1 -

I began writing this first day of week five on the first day of a brand new year. Two days before, I was confident in the coming year. I had well-prepared my business (which consumes most of my thinking). All my pricing information, client details, and portfolios were updated on all my websites. I had many goals already in place to be met within weeks. And I had generated an unexpected amount of buzz that left me excitedly anticipating the new year. But, personally, familiar sorrows crept up.

I've long battled the idea of how much is too much to share in the personal wait we've endured for a family. I talk about it with close friends, but even that is not at length. I don't want pity. And I don't want to make anyone uncomfortable. Because infertility is, by default, a topic that just...changes things. But God began speaking to me in very profound ways (which I shared in the introduction), and I've struggled with how to make those things line up with this study. The idea of suffering and affliction is not the kind of topic anyone can pick up at anytime and have it resonate in their spirit. But I can't be studying one thing and teaching another. And I feel God's nudging to stop resisting and start being even more vulnerable than I already have been. So this week, we make a shift.

Today's study began by accident. I knew I wanted to teach on contentment this week. I had the subject. Then God provided the material. Earlier today, I was perusing the wonders of Facebook and saw yet another pregnancy announcement. In recent years, I've found that I spend a lot of January bracing myself emotionally for February. The month we decided it was time for me to stop taking the pill. At the time of writing this, the six year anniversary was right around the corner. As I read of another friend rejoicing in another pregnancy, the pangs in my heart brought fresh tears to my eyes.

Out of pure curiosity, I went to blueletterbible.org and typed in the word "pang". There were no results in the King James version. So I went to biblegateway.com and typed in the same word. My last search on the site happened to be in the Amplified version, so the results displayed ten verses in that particular version. I was amazed as I perused the verses and almost laughed because of the subject matter I was pursuing this week.

Out of the ten verses listed, six of them referenced the pangs of childbirth.

I literally wrote in my prayer journal: *"we're darned if we do and we're darned if we don't."* With the abundance of conception, there is pain. And there is pain in the absence of it. Women that can't have children long for them. And women that have an abundance of children long for the quiet care-free days couples without children enjoy. What we really need across the baord is contentment. With our without. In plenty and in want. *Lord, in any circumstance, please just teach me how to be content!* The verse we'll begin looking at this week approaches this topic - not only regarding conception, but also in regards to marriage, which is where we left off last week.

Go to Genesis 3. Read verse 16, then write it here: _____
_____
_____

The story of Genesis 3 is, according to Matthew Henry, *"perhaps as sad a story (all things considered) as any we have in all the Bible. In the foregoing chapters we have had the pleasant view of the holiness and happiness of our first parents, the grace and favour of God, and the peace and beauty of the whole creation, all good, very good; but here the scene is altered. We have here an account of the sin and misery of our first parents, the wrath and curse of God against them, the peace of the creation disturbed, and its beauty stained and sullied, all bad, very bad."*

Verse 16 finds Eve receiving her punishment from God for her sin in the Garden of Eden. I began studying the verse like I always do - with the Hebrew Lexicon. And if you translate the verse according to the original Hebrew definitions, you can literally say it this way: *"I will increase greatly the increase of your sorrow..."* Fantastic.

The result of Eve's sin was not only pain in childbirth, but also in conception. Or the lack of it.

Go to blueletterbible.org, look up the word "thy sorrow", and write the definition here: _____
_____

Within the Gesenius' Hebrew-Chaldee Lexicon defintion, there is a cross-reference given for Psalm 147:3. Go read it.

This isn't portrayed in the actual verse, and wasn't written this way, but we can put some pieces together and see God's heart in a very dramatic way here. If you include the verse from Psalm 147 that was referenced in the Hebrew definition of "thy sorrow", you can add a paranthetical statement to this verse given in Genesis.

God is a holy God. He *must* punish sin because He is just. But He is also a God of grace and mercy. So I loved it when I wrote it this way in my prayer journal:

"I will increase greatly the increase of your sorrow (but I heal the brokenhearted and bind up their sorrows)."

Read Job 5:18, then write it here: _____
_____
_____

He wounds. And He heals. He kills. And He makes alive. (Deuteronomy 32:39, 1 Samuel 2:6-7)

The same idea is seen in Isaiah 30:26: *"Moreover, the light of the moon will be like the light of the sun, and the light of the sun will be sevenfold, like the light of seven days [concentrated in one], in the day that the Lord binds up the hurt of His people, and heals their wound [inflicted by Him because of their sins]." (Amplified version)*

Go back to Psalm 147:3, and look up the word for "and bindeth up" on blueletterbible.org, paying attention to the tense of the word. Write the definition here: _____

Reading further in the Gesenius Lexicon provides an even clearer picture of the intent of the word: *"spoken of a miner stopping off the water from flowing into his pits"*.

Think back to week one when we were talking about bitterness. Do you remember studying Exodus 15, where God made the bitter waters sweet? I thought of that again when I read the definition above. I imagined a frantic miner desperately trying to turn off the water source flooding his pits. Once the water is stopped, he's got to do something about the water that's already gotten in. Personally, I thought of the water in my current proverbial pit being rivers of sorrow. *How in the world do I drain all this?*

And then I found this verse tucked in the middle of a hymn from 1787:

"When through the deep waters, I call thee to go,
the rivers of sorrow shall not overflow;
for I will be with thee, thy trouble to bless,
and sanctify to thee thy deepest distress."
(How Firm a Foundation)

He makes the bitter waters sweet. Every time. We just have to choose to allow Him to. And in doing so, we have to want them to be sweet. Too often, in the struggle to find contentment, we hold onto the pain associated with not having what we want. It's a bizarre habit of human nature that I will never understand. And forever fight against.

I'll leave you with this quote from Streams in the Desert for January 1:
"We cannot see what loss, sorrow, and trials are accomplishing. We need only to trust. The Father comes near to take our hand and lead us on our way today."

Where do you need to begin easing into contentment? Begin the journey in your prayer journal.

There's no time like the present.

TREASURES *of* DARKNESS

WEEK 5: CONTENTMENT

- DAY 2 -

I sat down today still thinking about what we studied yesterday, letting it roll around in my brain. I couldn't get past the idea that, as Eve's punishment for sin (which directly affects every woman today), God greatly multiplied her sorrow. I looked up Genesis 3:16 in a handful of different commentaries and was not all that surprised to see that most of them summarized the verse into two parts: her pain in childbirth, and her desire for her husband (which we'll look at tomorrow). However, when I read it, I see *three* distinct punishments, especially after studying the words in the original Hebrew text.

As I thought on yesterday's study, I couldn't help but think of the 1 Peter 3:7 (which we didn't actually study last week, but provides the perfect segway into this week).

Read 1 Peter 3:7, and then write it here: _____
_____
_____

I'll be honest: I read a lot of cross-references to this verse, as well as a lot of commentaries - particularly in regards to the weaker vessel. I didn't like what they had to say. And that's probably just my pride stepping in. But the reality remains:
- Eve was deceived.
- She chose to partake of the forbidden fruit.
- She convinced Adam to join her in her sin.
- As a consequence, she was made subject to her husband.
- Because of that, women are inherently weaker. Like it or not.

After digging and digging for something that could tie the idea of the weaker vessel back to Genesis 3:16, I came up empty, and decided to move on to the last part of the verse. But then I saw something interesting. As I looked at the Hebrew words on blueletterbible.org, I noticed that there were two different renderings for the word "sorrow". We looked up the first one (*'itstsabown*) yesterday. The second is in reference to the pain of child birth. I clicked on the second word for "sorrow", and the light bulb went off.

Write the definition for *'etseb* here: _____
_____

Did you notice the first sentence in the Gesenus Lexicon? *(1) an earthen vessel.* I knew I was in the ballpark of where

I started, but couldn't find the connection. And, again, I followed the rabbit trail of cross references. It wasn't pretty. Look up the following verses and write them in the spaces provided below:

Jeremiah 22:28 _____
_____

Psalm 31:12 _____
_____

Hosea 8:8 _____
_____

God makes some vessels of gold and silver, and some of clay. The former is inherently stronger than the latter. Unfortunately, as women, we just happened to be created as the latter. (And literally created later - *after* Adam.)

The earthen vessel. The dirty, not shiny, certainly not pretty, weak vessel. All because Eve took a bite of an apple. It seems all doom and gloom. But remember the paranthetical statement we added to the first part of Genesis 3:16? There is always a "but" with God.

Read 2 Timothy 2:20-21 and write the verse here: _____
_____
_____
_____
_____

And finally, read Romans 9:20-23.

I don't know about you, but I'm incredibly thankful that He chooses to turn earthen vessels into vessels of mercy.

As women, we are the weaker vessel. That's something we will always fight against. In our marriages. In our emotions and hormones. In the workplace. But, in His mercy, He will use our weakness for His glory. Just like the altar of incense we studied in week two, He'll take our earthen vessels and dip them in pure gold. Covering us without and within with His Spirit. Sanctifying us and making us useful for Himself.

What Satan intended for our ruin, God used for His glory. May we take whatever sorrow, trial, affliction, or pain that seems to be greatly multiplied in our lives and allow Him to use them to make known the riches of His glory through these vessels of mercy. Because He prepared them beforehand for glory. Let's not allow Satan to use them as weapons against us.

TREASURES of DARKNESS

WEEK 5: CONTENTMENT

- DAY 3 -

We're going to pick up today right where we left off yesterday in Genesis 3:16, looking at part three of a three-part punishment given to Eve after her sin in the Garden of Eden.

Read the last part of verse 16 and write it here: _____

_____

You know what's next: go to blueletterbible.org and click on the phrase "and thy desire". Write the definition here:
_____

When God speaks of Eve's desire for her husband, He speaks of a craving. The root word provides a picture that literally means stretching out after something. Click on the phrase "and he shall rule". Write the definition here:
_____

I dug further in the Gesenius' Hebrew-Chaldee Lexicon and found an interesting definition tucked away in the middle of the section: *"that of judging, forming an opinion, which is nearly allied to the notion of ordering or ruling"*

Because of sin, woman was made inferior to man. I know the word "inferior" might have made some of you stop in your tracks. And not in a good way. But stick with me on this. When she ate the apple that they were both forbidden to eat, Eve proved that her ability to make sound decisions and judgements was in question. As a result, Adam was to step in. Continually. Present active participle. I found it interesting that the definition for "rule" specifically included the idea of forming an opinion - something that most women take offense to at one time or another in their marriage. Not being heard. Not getting their way. The dreaded idea of submission that we studied last week.

I love Matthew Henry's commentary: *"The entrance of sin has made that duty [of wives being subject to their own husbands] a punishment, which otherwise it would not have been. If man had not sinned, he would always have ruled with wisdom and love; and, if the woman had not sinned, she would always have obeyed with humility and meekness; and then the dominion would have been no grievance: but our own sin and folly make our yoke heavy. If Eve had not eaten forbidden fruit herself, and tempted her husband to eat it, she would never have complained of her subjection; therefore it ought never to be complained of, though harsh; but sin must be complained of, that made it so. Those wives who not only despise and disobey their husbands, but domineer over them, do not consider that they not only violate a divine law, but thwart a divine sentence."*

Going back to the word "desire", flip one chapter over to Genesis 4 and read verse 7.

At this point, we know of our place in marriage - whether or not we like it. We know of the specific punishment given to us as women back in the very beginning of time. Satan would love nothing better than to hold it over us. Twist it for us. Turn it into the very apple he gave to Eve, and tempt us to bite out of it.

Read 1 Peter 5:8, and then write the verse here: _____
_____

I love how the Amplified version translates the same verse: *"Be well balanced (temperate, sober of mind), be vigilant and cautious at all times; for that enemy of yours, the devil, roams around like a lion roaring [in fierce hunger], seeking someone to seize upon and devour."* As women, we can especially pay heed to the warning to be well balanced, temperate, and sober of mind.

How easy it is to fix our eyes on what we want, forgetting what we've already been given. We only see the children that we don't have and forget about the incredible husband that we do. We can't get past the fact that our husband always makes the decisions and forget that he also has to carry the weight of that responsibility.

We suffer from want when we can rest in contentment.

May we not resist the divine sentence God has given. May we not try to thwart our husband's authority. May we not manipulate him or try to domineer over him. The reality is this punishment was given to Eve generations upon generations ago. Who are we to think that God will change it for us?

God, may we find joy in the divine sentence You've given. And contentment in submission.

TREASURES *of* DARKNESS

WEEK 5: CONTENTMENT

- DAY 4 -

I've been sitting here staring at a blank screen for 20 minutes. I'm out of my routine, at a coffee shop in Corvallis, Oregon waiting for yet another chemotherapy treatment with Shawna, and I'm thinking about contentment. Yet somehow, the verses I'm reading aren't quite hitting it. I'm not thinking about the type of contentment that fights the daily pull down the all-to0-familiar-road of materialism. I'm thinking about deep soul-satisfying contentment. Contentment not just in His provision *but in His sovereignty*. Contentment when His sovereignty doesn't make sense.

Contentment in waiting. Contentment in obedience. Contentment in His divine plan.

I think this sort of contentment applies on a much deeper level of hurt and loneliness that not many people like to talk about. Contentment in the unfulfilled want of a lifelong partner in a longer-than-I-thought season of singleness. Contentment in the disenchantment of marriage, when the fairytale is over, reality sets in, and you find yourself with a husband who isn't exactly what you hoped for. Contentment in years of periods when all you want it a baby. Contentment in cancer and disease and scans with heart-wrenching results.

Contentment in unfulfilled dreams and unanswered prayers.

I just pulled up a list of verses in which the word "content" is used in scripture. The first one I looked up is in reference to Proverbs 6:34-45, speaking of adultery. At first glance, this particular verse doesn't necessarily apply. But upon digging deeper, it's unquestionable. When I looked up the Hebrew definition for "content" (also translated "be appeased" in the KNJV, and "satisfied" in the Amplified), I knew I was on the right track:

To breathe after.

There it is - the theme we've seen woven throughout our study from the very beginning! Since I knew I was headed down the right path, I took a few minutes to look up each individual verse referenced in the Gesenius Lexicon to see what other insight I could gather. Look up the following verses and see if you can detect a pattern through them all:

Exodus 10:27
Leviticus 26:21
Deuteronomy 2:30
Deuteronomy 25:7
2 Samuel 13:14, 16

Psalm 81:12
Proverbs 1:24
Isaiah 30:9

What pattern, if any, did you notice? _____
_____

I found it interesting that each of the referenced verses included some sort of no-arguments decision. Stubbornness. No wiggle room. God hardening the heart of a king. A brother refusing to marry his deceased brother's wife. God's people refusing to listen to His word. A man refusing to set aside his jealousy. Israel walking contrary to God, refusing to obey Him. Amnon forcing himself on Tamar. Pharoah refusing to let God's people go. Counsel disdained. Rebuke refused. My way or the highway.

And then I read on in the Gesenius' Hebrew-Chaldee Lexicon. For the first time, I saw an entire definition form a complete word picture. The journey of contentment begins with a softening stubbornness.

To be willing towards anyone. To be willing in mind. To obey.

Isn't that just the way that the process of finding contentment goes? I have something I want. Something I feel absolutely entitled to. Something I was created for that I am being refused. I stomp my feet. Dig my heels in stubbornness and in want. I exhale and huff in frustration. Breathing after something that is just out of my reach. How long do we stand in stubbornness, refusing the walk down the path God has set before us?

Read Isaiah 1:19 and write the verse here: _____
_____

This is another case of *'abah*, the Hebrew word we've been studying. A promising case. Literally.

Matthew Henry talks about it this way: "*...subject your wills to the will of God, acquiesce in that, and give up yourselves in all things to be ruled by him who is infinitely wise and good...He does not say, 'If you be perfectly obedient,' but, 'If you be willingly so;" for, if there be a willing mind, it is accepted."*

That last part is like water to my soul. Contentment is not an easy thing to settle into. It's more of a habit you must train your mind into. I'm so thankful that, like in all things with God, there is grace. We don't need to be perfectly obedient. We just need to be willing. He'll fill in the rest of the gap.

Spend the rest of your time today praying about specific areas in your life where you recognize the need for contentment. Confess any stubbornness or sin in resisting God's sovereign plan for your life. And pray for the strength to breathe after Him - even if it means turning your back on your dreams for awhile.

TREASURES *of* DARKNESS

WEEK 5: CONTENTMENT

- DAY 5 -

We've made it to the end of another week, and this journey has been so exciting for me. I have no clue where it will end. And I'm so thankful you're discovering these things with me as I discover them. Thank you for being willing to explore and wrestle through these thoughts with me. And for allowing me to be vulnerable.

I can't stop thinking today about contentment and obedience. The two are powerfully interconnected and inherently dependent on each other. While you can be obedient without necessarily feeling content, contentment is a matter of obedience. And God is incredibly honored by it.

I'm also thinking about the definition we looked up yesterday - the idea of breathing after a thing in the context we looked at yesterday. Wanting it. Huffing because you can't have it. Facing it. Reaching for it. Longing after it. Or, you can breathe *after* it. Letting go of the burden and sighing a breath of relief. This might be silly, but I want you to physcially try both.

Exhale out in a huff as you would if you were frustrated about something.

Now exhale a long sigh of relief.

The Hebrew word *"naphach"* means to breathe. To disperse, or cast away by blowing. As I read that I sat here for a moment, took some deep breaths, and breathed out slowly as if I were blowing the seeds of a dandelion into the wind. The release of the thing you want so badly as a prayer to heaven. Read the following verses and also write them down:

Psalm 23:1 _____
_____

Psalm 34:10 _____
_____

Psalm 84:11 _____
_____

It's imperative to keep in mind that, in the process of want, we idealize the delivery of the thing desired. A single woman longs to be married, not knowing the submission struggle that awaits in a marriage relationship. A married woman longs for a child, not knowing that she might face losing that same child years down the road.

Shawna and I were talking about contentment this morning, and the pain that lies in the struggle of it. The reality is: life is full of pain. There is pain in unanswered prayer, but also in the answered ones. We will always be disappointed. Expectations will always fail. Husbands will let us down. Friends will betray. Children will disobey. Tragedies happen. Health fails. In all scenarios, we must be content. We must remember that if He is witholding, the thing being held back must not be good for us. And, when He does give, we must it receive with open hands. Ready to hand it right back to Him.

Read Genesis 22:1-19.

When Eve had her first child, she replied with *"I have acquired from the Lord."* (Gen. 4:1) When Hannah had her first child, she replied with *"I give him to the Lord."* (1 Sam. 1:28) Abraham and Sarah longed for a child for practically their entire lives. And the one thing they longed for, waited for, and loved more than anything else... God asked for back.

God honored Abraham because he didn't keep his miracle son. He didn't refuse the drastic step of faith God required of him. He didn't keep Isaac back for himself. He didn't deny God the most treasured thing that God gave to him. He was ready to give back what was given to him.

Contentment displays obedience. And it necessitates surrender.

Read Philippians 4:10-13 and write it here: _____
_____
_____
_____
_____
_____

What are you whitholding from God that you're afraid to lose? Spend some time praying in your journal for that tight grip to be loosened and released to Him.

TREASURES OF DARKNESS

THIS WEEK'S NUGGET:

In all their affliction, He was afflicted, and the Angel of His Presence saved them; in His love and in His pity He redeemed them; and He bore them and carried them all the days of old.

Isaiah 63:9

TREASURES of DARKNESS

WEEK 6: UNDERSTANDING AFFLICTION

- INTRODUCTION -

As I write this, my soul is tired. And battle weary. Tired of being strong. Tired of continually believing. Tired of hope followed by periods and fervent prayer followed with scans that are always just a little worse than the last. I'm just... tired. I was joking with a girlfriend last night that my spiritual muscles are on the thirty-day shred. It's beginning to look like the thirty-*year* shred. And then I read Spurgeon. And Psalm 35.

"**Many** are the **afflictions** of the **righteous**. <u>**But the LORD**</u> **delivers** him out of them all. **He guards all his bones**, not one is broken." (Psalm 35: 19-20, as written and emphasized in my journal)

God, through this ongoing trial of waiting for a family, and waiting for healing for Shawna, may I not lost faith. Not <u>ever</u>. And when I feel my faith falter, may I beeline straight to Your presence. May I neither lose hope. Nor love. Spurgeon calls these **bones of character**: *'Nay so far from losing these bones of character, they have gained in strength and energy. I have more knowledge, more experience, more patience, more stability than I had before the trials came. Not even my joy has been destroyed. Many a bruise have I had by sickness, bereavement, depression, slander, and opposition; but the bruise has been healed, and there is no compound fracture of a bone, not even a simple one. The reason is not far to seek. If we trust in the LORD, He keeps all our bones; and if He keeps them, we may be sure that not one of them is broken.* **Come my heart, do not sorrow.** *Thou art smarting, but there are no bones broken.* **Endure hardness and bid defiance to fear.**[1]

I began to think of bones broken in scripture. Or, rather, bones unbroken. The Passover lamb in Exodus 12 was to be free of any blemish or broken bones. In John 19, when Jesus was taken off the cross, they did not break His legs (though it was customary). And in 2 Corinthians 4, Paul points out that though we are hard pressed on every side, *we are not crushed.*

"**All my bones shall say**, 'LORD, who is like You, delivering the poor from him who is too strong for him?" (Psalm 35:10)

That verse you just read is one of only two places in scripture attributing exulting joy to the bones - it's typically associated with the vital organs. We can always tell how our intestines are affected by our emotions - butterflies in the stomach, etc. But you can't tell how your bones are doing as easily. And if you can, it's typically bad news. The moment the cancer entered Shawna's bones...she knew. You can feel physical deterioration in the bones. Strengthing in the bones? You can't. Likewise, "we have no consciousness of the bones becoming sympathetically sensitive. The expression therefore is highly practical, and indicates that the joy intended would be far beyond ordinary and common delight, it

---

[1] Charles Spurgeon, *Faith's Checkbook: December 19th (Moody Publishers, 1987).*

would be so profound that even the most callous part of the human frame would partake of it." [2]

How true and necessary this is. When I'm facing deply difficult trials and emotional afflictions that sap any feeling of joy, I can remember the words: **all my bones shall say, 'LORD, who is like You?'**

The second place in scripture that joy is attributed to the bones? Psalm 51:8. A prayer by David, seeking comfort at the right time *from the right source.* The verse is speaking specifically of sin and salvation, but how often do I need to hear joy and gladness to drown out the sorrow playing on repeat in my brain?

Throughout scripture, a broken bone is a symbolic representation of sin. And then it hit me. So hard and so fast that I couldn't get the prayer out fast enough. Or emphatically enough. **LORD, may my affliction never become my sin.** *May this affliction never become a stronghold of sorrow. May it not rob me of my joy. Nor break my faith. Even when I don't "feel" it, LORD, may my bones still cry out in joy to you.*

"The LORD will guide you continually, and satisfy your soul in drought, and **strengthen your bones**; *you shall be like a watered garden, and like a spring of water, whose waters do not fail." (Isaiah 58:11)*

LORD, give my bones rest - rest from the sorrow. Rest from the pain. Give rest to my weary bones. And be my joy.

---

[2] Charles Spurgeon, Treasury of David: *thoughts suggested by a passage in "Biblical Psychology," by Franz Delitzsch.*

TREASURES *of* DARKNESS

WEEK 6: UNDERSTANDING AFFLICTION

- DAY 1 -

Welcome to another week of digging deeply into God's word. The fact that you're even reading this is a good sign. Six weeks in, and you're still invested. I'm so thankful. We introduced this week with a continuation of last week's conversation on the bones of character, which led us to 1 Samuel 1 - the story of Hannah, and how God breathed new life into her nearly dried-out faith. After spending time last week studying contentment, I think we're perfectly prepared to embark on this week.

As always, I had an idea of where I wanted to begin the week. And God provided the confirmation right away that I was on the right path. My prayer journal from 2010 provided the backbone to this study, and I referenced it this morning to begin my week. It was long before Shawna's diagnosis and I began really thinking about sovereignty and suffering. Providence and affliction. Contentment and waiting. For twenty minutes, I flipped through page after hand-written page, digging for what I knew was there. Somewhere. And then I found it: August 23, 2010. Even better? The day before was five pages worth of pouring my heart out and studying 1 Samuel 1. The story of Hannah. One woman's anguish. And God's incredible answer to her desperate prayer.

I want to begin this week looking at Isaiah 63:9. Read the verse, then write it here: _____
_____
_____
_____

You know what happens next. Both the NKJV and KJV use the words "affliction" and "afflicted". Begin by looking up the phrase "in all their affliction" on blueletterbible.org and write the definition here: _____
_____

Did you notice the part where it said "rival wife"? I thought that was incredibly specific, and especially interesting on the heels of what we talked about together with Hannah, vexed by her husband's other wife. And then I laughed because, as expected, God confirmed I was on the right track. The definition literally referenced 1 Samuel 1:6.

Have you ever had a rival? A competitor within the same market of your business? Someone you're continually trying to outdo? If so, give a brief story here. _____
_____
_____

I can pretty much guarantee that there was some talk involved. Gossip. A little dig here and there. Maybe more. The same Hebrew root word used for the word "affliction" is also used in Psalm 42:10. I think you'll find another correlation to our introduction in this verse. Look it up and then write it here: _____
_____

Spurgeon has a poignant commentary on this verse, that also brings us all the way back to week one of our study: *"Cruel mockeries cut deeper than the flesh, they reach the soul as though a rapier [a slender, sharply pointed sword, ideally used for thrusting attacks] were introduced between the ribs to prick the heart...the tongue cuts to the bone, and its wounds are hard to cure."*

I imagine that's exactly what Hannah was experiencing when she ran to find refuge at the doors of the tabernacle in 1 Samuel 1, her rival wife's voice echoing in her ears. The constant digs that Elkanah must love her more - after all, look how many children they have together. And it's that sort of affliction that Isaiah 63:9 is referring to.

Read Psalm 31:10 and write it here: _____
_____
_____

There are a couple different schools of thought as to the interpretation of Isaiah 63:9. One commentary interprets the verse as *"'hardly an affliction had befallen [the Israelites] when the Angel of His presence saved them' or, as best suits the parallelism, 'in all their straits there was no straitness in His goodness to them.'"*[1] In other words, the affliction led them to a narrow, constricted place. We were in the midst of some turmoil a handful of years ago that found us getting out of town just to get away from it. For the few days we were gone, we could breathe. But once the trip was over, and we began making our way home, the claustrophobic feeling began creeping in. Yet, in all of the constriction of affliction, His goodness isn't limited. Tightened. Narrow. Restricted.

Another interpretation comes with the change of just one letter in the Hebrew, and the entire verse is transformed to read *"'In all their affliction there was no (utterly overwhelming) affliction.' The idea is that the very property of their affliction was so altered by the grace of God sanctifying it to them for their good, the rigor of it was so balanced with mercies, that it was in effect no affliction."*[2]

The grace of God and the joy of His presence negates the effect of afflictions. In all our afflictions, He is afflicted. He takes them upon Himself, trading our ashes for His beauty. Trading our mourning for His oil of joy. Trading our spirit of heaviness for His garment of praise. That we may be called flourishing trees of righteousness when it looks like we're languishing (Isaiah 61:2).

Spend the rest of your time this morning reading the remainder of Isaiah 63:9. Pray through the verse in your journal, remembering that He doesn't send someone else to help you. He does it Himself. Because nobody is as intimately acquainted with your thoughts, emotions, and struggles as He is.

[1] *Jamieson, Fausset, Brown, A Commentary: Critical, Practical and Explanatory, on the Old & New Testaments (Jerome B. Names & Co., 1884), pg 283*
[2] *Matthew Henry, The Comprehensive Commentary on the Holy Bible: Isaiah LXIII, (The Brattleboro Typographic Company, 1837), pg 486*

TREASURES *of* DARKNESS

WEEK 6: UNDERSTANDING AFFLICTION

- DAY 2 -

I want to take some time this morning to explore what, exactly, affliction is. When I first began exploring and praying through this theme in 2010, I was well aware of the negative connotation I had grown to associate with suffering and affliction. I never wanted to say the word, or apply it to myself, because so many people seemed to use it as their emotional crutch. But really, every single one of us encounters affliction at one time or another.

According to a resource I found online about the doctrine of suffering, affliction *"is a tool God uses to get our attention and to accomplish His purposes in our lives. It is designed to build our trust in the Almighty...it forces us to turn from trust in our own resources to living by faith in God's."* [1]

For the longest time, I associated suffering and affliction only with persecution. In reality, it's anything that disturbs our peace. Anything that hurts or irritates. The article continues: *"It's designed to make us think. It's a tool God uses to get our attention and to accomplish His purposes in our lives in a way that would never occur without the trial or irritation."*

List some examples of affliction that you can think of, big or small: _____
_____
_____
_____
_____
_____
_____
_____

Affliction can be as simple as a sore throat or as complex as cancer. It can be the overwhelming loss of someone close to you. It can be a personal failure or disappointment. It can be a circulating rumor that's damaging your reputation and bringing grief or anxiety (whether or not it's true). It can be anything as small as a mosquito bite or as large as facing a lion's den (Daniel 6).

Read Psalm 119:71, and write the verse here: _____
_____

---

[1] J. Hampton Keathley, III, *The Doctrine of Suffering*

"God visited David with affliction that he might learn God's statutes; and the intention was answered: the afflictions had contributed to the improvement of his knowledge and grace." (Matthew Henry) The word "learn" in Hebrew refers to training cattle. Are you familiar with Acts 9:5? It's in the middle of Paul's conversion story when God literally stopped him on the road, on the way to physically threaten the lives of Christians and told him *"it is hard for you to kick against the goads"*. Goads are iron pricks used for urging oxen. It's futile to push against them - all they'll do is hurt you, and the rancher will get his oxen where he wants them to go eventually anyway.

Our natural tendency when we're in affliction is to kick back. If we're hurt, injure back. Lash out. Cry out in pain. Do whatever it takes to make it stop. Instead, God wants us to relax into Him, stop resisting it, and allow the affliction to train us in the knowledge of His word. His mercy. His grace. And His comfort. Like cattle, we need to be trained. And sometimes that takes painful measures.

William Seeker is a theologian from the mid-1600s, and has this to say regarding Psalm 119:71: *"There are some things good but not pleasant, as sorrow and affliction. Sin is pleasant, but unprofitable; and sorrow is profitable but unpleasant. Some Christians resemble those children who will learn their books no longer than while the rod is on their backs [teachers - remember this is the 1600s]. It is well known that by the greatest affliction the Lord has sealed the sweetest instruction... the purest gold is the most pliable."*

All this really goes back to what we studied last week on contentment. Patiently waiting things out, and trusting God through the entire process. I said it last week, and I'll say it again: **I don't ever want my affliction to become my sin.**

What does the first part of Isaiah 53:7 say? _____
_____

That verse is specifically referring to Jesus not opening His mouth in complaint or in resistance to the oppression and affliction He was suffering. Instead, He *did* open His mouth to His Father in raw emotion and vulnerability in the Garden of Gethsemane. "Nevertheless," He said, *"not My will, but THY will be done."*

The night before Shawna's first chemotherapy treatment, we sat on her couch. She was anxiety-ridden and fearful about what was to come and the war her body was about to endure. Through tears, and with a shaky voice, she prayed those words. *"If there is any way we can skip over this...if there is some way I don't have to go tomorrow...if it is Your will, PLEASE take this cup from me ... Nevertheless, LORD, not my will, but Yours be done."*

Is there an affliction you're currently facing? If so, spend the rest of your time telling God about it in your journal. And then use your concordance or the tools we've used throughout our study to find verses that pertain to it. Turn them into prayers, allowing God to use your affliction to teach you His promises.

TREASURES *of* DARKNESS

WEEK 6: UNDERSTANDING AFFLICTION

- DAY 3 -

Have I told you yet how excited I am that you're doing this study with me? The fact that you're exploring this brand new world of raw vulnerability and discovery with me is humbling. I now know the theme of this study with full confidence. It took six weeks for me to be fully assured of it, but since the word "breathe" showed up yet again in the process of my studying, I can't argue with it. Breathe. *Just breathe.* Through tough conversations. And disciplining children. And bickering with your husband. And suffering and loss and blessing and joy. Just. Breathe.

I feel like Jacob in Genesis 28 when God meets him dramatically in a dream. *"Surely God is in this place, and I did not know it."* When I started writing the homework for this study, it was more or less a filler. Something to give my small group that they could do throughout the week. To help cultivate the habit of seeking God's heart every single morning if they didn't already. I had no idea what He really had in store. One little step of obedience has turned into an incredible, unexpected journey. So far, my feet aren't tired. So we'll keep walking forward.

We're going to spend the remainder of our week looking at the different types of affliction. The first is what we've already been looking at: the standard calamities of everyday life. Big or small. Whether they last for days or years - it's all of the same importance to God. Years ago, before her own cancer battle was even a thought in her mind, Shawna was talking with a dear woman at our church who had lost her husband to cancer. They were sharing stories, and Shawna suddenly felt that what had been a large obstacle in her life at the time drastically paled in comparison with what Cindy had endured. As she expressed that thought, Cindy interrupted her. *"My trial then is no less than your own now,"* she said. Because when we're in the midst of it, the struggle is difficult. And very real. And God looks upon all afflictions the same. We just seek Him a little bit more intensively through some of them. *LORD, may we never diminish the afflictions of another because it seems light or trivial to us.*

As you know my own personal story, you will understand how intrigued I was to see that three of the first four verses I read as I studied the word "affliction" occurred in Genesis - particularly in the context of God providing a child as an answer to seeing or hearing the prayer of a woman enduring affliction. But it's not given to the person you might expect.

Read Genesis 16:11 and then write the verse here: _____
_____
_____

In the previous chapter (Genesis 15), God made a covenant with Abraham. *"Look now toward heaven, and count the stars if you are able to number them,"* He told him. *"So shall your descendants be."* And we read that Abraham *believed* the LORD, and He accounted it to him for righteousness. Then ten years went by (Genesis 3:16).

Sarah, Abraham's wife, had yet to bear a child. And while she recognized God's providence in the restraint of it (16:2), she didn't keep her eyes locked on it. And her desire for the one thing she had been denied now for ten years and counting got the better of her. So she gave her maid to her husband and, almost immediately, Hagar became pregnant. The aftermath wasn't pretty. Hagar tormented Sarah with the new life she obtained so quickly making Sarah strongly resent the very thing she forced, and "dealt harshly" with Hagar - likely requiring much more work out of her maid and humiliating her while she was at it. So, Hagar fled. And God met her on the road. The fact is: Hagar made a choice to lay with Abraham. She chose to hold it over Sarah's head that she had conceived. She chose to flee and protect her pride. But God still saw her affliction. *"When we have brought ourselves into distress by our own sin, yet God has not forsaken us."* (Matthew Henry)

The same thing happened with a woman named Leah. She was the unfortunate victim of her father's scheme with Jacob, who was in love with her sister (Rachel). He served her dad faithfully for seven years for the chance to marry her. Laban gave him Leah instead. Though she didn't hold it over Rachel's head - she still suffered privately. More quietly than Hagar. Read Genesis 29:31-32 and write the words in your prayer journal.

He knows our sorrows. He sees our wounds - even when we don't talk about them. Good, bad, or ugly, He still has compassion because He is merciful. I also want to point out that both women in these two different circumstances were the lesser loved women. God shows His love in dramatic ways just when we need to see it most. Sometimes that's showing up in the midst of affliction when our faith is faltering. Or when we don't even have an ounce of faith left. And sometimes that's allowing us to seek Him diligently through the affliction. Instead of meeting us physically, He meets us in more subtle ways. Like providing small, consistent trailmarkers over a span of weeks. Repeating words or verses from various unrelated sources. If we're looking, He is there.

We'll end by looking at Joseph in Genesis 42. Up to this point, Joseph had endured quite a bit of affliction, most of which was out of his control (much like Hagar and Leah). His brothers (ironically, the descendants of Hagar's child from Genesis 16) were jealous and sold him to the Ishmaelites for twenty shekels of silver - about one hundred dollars. For awhile, he was a slave. Then he was thrown in prison for a misunderstanding involving his master's wife. But soon, things began to turn around. And we find Joseph saying similar words in Genesis 42 that were spoken to Hagar, and that Leah spoke of upon her son's birth.

Read Genesis 41:52 and write the verse here: _____
_____

Just like Job, God allowed Joseph to rejoice in the blessings in the latter part of his life and forget about the miseries of the former part. God is faithful to provide after-comforts if we can just be patient in our affliction. In His kindness, He gives treasures of darkness. Affliction is never futile. And God always provides the comfort.

Finish your time by praying through Psalm 119:50 in your journal. If you aren't experiencing affliction now, tuck this away in the back of your mind. You might need to have it on hand some day.

TREASURES *of* DARKNESS

WEEK 6: UNDERSTANDING AFFLICTION

- DAY 4 -

We're finishing off the week looking at the different types of affliction. Yesterday we looked at the standard calamities of the everyday. The sort of things that happen just because they are part of life or the result of another person's actions that directly affect you. A more appropriate perspective would be recognizing His providence acting in your life. I love that the Spirit is specifically called our comforter in John 14:26, literally giving us *"divine strength needed to enable [us] to undergo trials and persecutions on behalf of the divine kingdom."* We'll look more at that tomorrow. Today, we'll be looking at the second type of affliction: disciplinary.

I spent a couple of hours studying all the different words in scripture used for affliction, afflict, or afflicted. While there are fifteen different words for affliction, there are only seven for afflict. The most interesting part? They're all used in the Old Testament. Read Lamentations 3:31-33, and write the verses here: _____

_____

_____

_____

_____

When I was 19, I found myself in the throws of depression. The same season I mentioned in day four of week two. I was two years into the same emotionally-shredding relationship that fueled my mirror obsession. We had only officially dated for six months, but I couldn't pry myself away from him for still another year. I made choices that directly contradicted my faith and my convictions, and I was living in the midst of the repercussions of my sin. Every morning on the walk into my bathroom, I looked at a verse that I had written on an index card and tacked above the door: *"No discipline seems pleasant at the time, but painful. Later on, however, it produces a harvest of righteousness and peace for those who have been trained by it." (Hebrews 12:11, NIV)*

I knew what was happening. I recognized my sin in the circumstance. And I knew I had to simply wait it out - as long as it took - and pray that I would be trained by the consequences of my choices. It's a comforting thing to know that though He cast us down, He does *not* cast us off. He's not disowning us. Rather, He's a father disciplining His child.

Read Isaiah 48:10, and write the verse here: _____

_____

_____

The term "furnace of affliction" is an extreme one. The furnace described is one used to separate precious metal from ore, and the silver won't even begin to melt until the temperature reaches a scorching temperature of 1435° F. However, God doesn't use the full refining silver process with us. If that were the case, we would always be in the furnace because we are inherently sinful beings. The dross is never fully separated from us. Though He does discipline, and often times it isn't pleasurable, it's thankfully not with the most extreme severity. It just so happens that He uses affliction to turn up the heat to purge the sin.

Describe a time when you knew God was disciplining you as a direct result of sin: _____
_____
_____
_____

In Ezekiel 22, God sees Israel as solid dross in a furnace with no redeeming qualities or any hint of silver in sight. Book after book after book in the Old Testament shows God patiently waiting for His people to fully yield to Him. Yet they still ran after idols, resisted His Word, despised His holy things and profaned His Sabbaths. They indulged in the lust of the flesh, the lust of the eyes, and the pride of life to excess. And He had enough. Read verses 17-22.

This is a classic case-in-point of disciplinary affliction. Proof that God doesn't mess around. Though He's patient and long-suffering, eventually - if we refuse to turn from our sin - He will give us over to it. Just like He did with Pharaoh in Exodus. Over and over, Pharaoh hardened his heart. Then finally, God hardened it for him. In Ezekiel 22:21, we see the breath of God used in a way that puts the fear of God in me. It reminds me that I truly am serving a Holy God and though I'm somewhat numb to sin, He is not. And He will not tolerate it.

Re-read verses 20 and 21. Then go to blueletterbible.org and look up the word "blow" that's used twice in those two verses. What word do you see right off the bat? _____

Another definition of the word is to value lightly. I can't help but think about where we started this study: talking about the breath of God giving us life. When we choose to indulge in sin, we're truly blowing Him off - pushing our Biblical values and convictions aside for temporary pleasures much like Esau trading his birthright for a bowl of soup (Genesis 25). If we belittle the very God that created us long enough, we will unfortunately face a judgement of fire. Or, we can allow affliction to discipline us. We can allow the chastisement of God train us. Refine us. Purify us. So much that it will leave a continual harvest of righteousness behind. Lesson learned.

I will leave you with Deuteronomy 16:3. The bread of affliction that's referred to here is unleavened bread - it wasn't necessarily the best tasting, and certainly not the easiest to digest. But it signified the heavy spirit of God's people in their slavery in Egypt, and the haste in which they came out.

Disciplinary affliction is only found in the Old Testament because the New Testament gives us Jesus, replacing the Passover meal with the Lord's Supper. *"And as they were eating, Jesus took bread, blessed and broke it, and gave it to the disciples and said, 'Take, eat; this is My body." (Matthew 26:26).*

Instead of judgement, we receive grace. Instead of God breathing the fire of His wrath, we have Jesus breathing His last breath, taking the punishment for our sin once and for all. *Oh LORD, may we not take that lightly.*

TREASURES *of* DARKNESS

WEEK 6: UNDERSTANDING AFFLICTION

- DAY 5 -

One day left, and this week is another one for the books! Let's begin by recapping what we've already looked at. What are the two types of affliction that we've already studied together?

1. _____
2. _____

Today, we're going to look at the third type of affliction - one that we can't possibly begin to even wrap our brains around in the comfortable culture we live in. One that is truly undeserved: suffering for Christ.

According to a report by an Italian sociologist in 2011, Christians are dying for their faith at the rate of one every five minutes. The January 2011 issue of the International Bulletin of Missionary Research reported the number of Christian martyrs per year peaked at around 160,000 in the year 2000, but since the cessation of hostilities in the Sudan it had fallen to around 100,000 per year. His estimate of 105,000 Christian martyrs in 2011,*"between 287 and 288 martyrs per day: twelve per hour, or one every five minutes,' was a conservative estimate."* [1]

In that same year, a Ugandan pastor was blinded in an attack: *"Islamic extremists attacked a Ugandan pastor outside his church near Kampala on Christmas Eve, leaving him blind in one eye. Umar Mulinde, the 37-year-old pastor of Gospel Life Church International in Namasuba, told Compass that he was returning to the church for a party with the congregation when a man approached him and called out, "Pastor, pastor." When Mulinde turned to look, several men poured acid on his face and back. Mulinde's face, neck and arms were severely burned and he lost sight in one eye. Mulinde had received several threats before the attack for his evangelism and opposition to Sharia courts in Uganda. In October 2011, Muslim leaders declared a fatwa on Mulinde, demanding his death."* [2]

Read 2 Timothy 1:8 and write the verse in your prayer journal.

2 Timothy is the last letter we have written by Paul, bound in chains in a prison in Rome for his faith. His last words of exhortation are to Timothy, his son in the faith across the sea in Ephesus. Most versions across the board use the word "suffering", with one exception. The KJV renders it as "affliction". Go to blueletterbible.org, look up the phrase "be thou partaker of the afflictions" and write the definition here: _____

This phrase that expresses suffering hardship for the benefit and furtherance of the gospel is only used once in scripture.

---

1   *The Church of England Newspaper, June 17, 2011 pg 1.*
2   *The Persecution Blog: VOM-USA Prayer Update for January 13, 2012*

And it got me thinking: *how does suffering further the gospel?* And then I thought of Jayden. I photographed her in the NICU when she was a little miracle newborn. Her parents were originally told she had less than a 5% chance of making it to term, and the prognosis later changed to a 50% chance of survival upon birth while they watched her underdeveloped lungs. Jayden beat all odds. With a waiting room full of praying friends from their church, and parents full of faith that Jayden would survive, she came out screaming with a full set of lungs. And when they anticipated she'd be in the NICU for up to twelve weeks, she went home in three. As I delivered the photographs from our time together at their house, her mom shared that because of Jayden's story, her doctor got saved.

Her suffering and fight to beat the odds furthered the gospel.

Then I thought of one of Josh's close friends from high school. Bart was Josh's tennis partner, and their friendship carried through to college where they were both involved in our college ministry. In June of 2002, Bart was one of a dozen passengers in a van on the way to fight a large wildfire in Colorado when the van crashed. Six of the passengers died, including Bart. The survivors of the accident remembered one specific detail about Bart on that trip: he was reading The Case for Christ when the accident happened. At his memorial service, we watched as dozens of people gave their lives to Christ because of Bart's example.

His suffering and the suffering of his family furthered the gospel.

Think of a time when you, or someone you know, suffered for the furtherance of the gospel: _____
_____
_____

Back to 2 Timothy. Ray Stedman describes Paul's words this way: *"He reminds Timothy that every Christian, without exception, is called to suffer for the gospel's sake. 'Oh,' you say, 'that isn't me. I don't suffer.' And I think sometimes we tend to feel we have been excluded from this. It may be because we always think of suffering as something physical - torture and thumb-screws and iron maidens and being torn apart on the rack, this sort of thing. Well, Christians do suffer in this way from time to time. In fact, the twentieth century is the most tortured Christian century of all. Did you know that? More Christians have been put to death for Christ's sake in this century than in any other century since the very beginning. But the suffering that is involved here is not only physical, it is mental as well. It is the kind of suffering we endure when somebody smiles knowingly and winks at our faith, or jibes at us, or laughs at us, or excludes us from an invitation list, or treats us with considerable and open disdain or contempt because we are a Christian; someone who pokes fun at a prayer meeting, or laughs at the Bible. We are to take this patiently, says the apostle. And as we react, not with anger or with disgust or vengeance, but quietly, patiently, as our Lord did, we guard the truth."* [3]

Spend the rest of your time in prayer, asking God in your journal to help you to be faithful and strong in the times you are called to suffer for Him. In big ways or small, He's honored when we stand up for our faith (a lot of times without words) and are unashamed of the gospel.

---

[3] *Ray Stedman, 2 Timothy 2: How Not To Collapse*

THIS WEEK'S NUGGET:

And the ransomed of the LORD shall return, and come to Zion with singing, with everlasting joy on their heads. They shall obtain joy and gladness, and sorrow and sighing shall flee away.

Isaiah 35:10

TREASURES *of* DARKNESS

WEEK 7: THANKFULNESS & JOY

- INTRODUCTION -

It was February 2011. Fresh from an amazing Mexican vacation with my husband, I made a spontaneous decision to attend a women's retreat. That very month marked the five year anniversary of going off the pill. I was attending the retreat because I wanted a release. To let down the walls. To talk about this struggle that I'd kept inside for so long. And maybe, just a little bit, to feel sorry for myself.

When I arrived to my room for the weekend, there were beds full of familiar, favorite faces. And there was one unfamiliar face. We were introduced, and I realized I had already known a little bit of her story. She was young. A brand new Christian. Unmarried. And pregnant.

It's not about you that still, small, pressing Voice whispered to me. So I swallowed the lump in my throat. And shoved my feel-sorry-for-me intentions. And smiled.

The next day, I made my way into the gym as a teaching session was scheduled to start. I was early. *I'm never early.* And I was alone. My unexpected roommate sat by herself at the end of the aisle, a handful of rows from the front. So I made my way to her. Sat down next to her. And began talking. I didn't bring up the pregnancy because I didn't want to make her uncomfortable. So we made small talk. *I'm not good at small talk.*

It didn't take long before she said she was pregnant and pointed to her growing belly. And, without missing a beat, she also said she wasn't married. Airing out her shame before I had the opportunity to ask.

"*Who cares?!*" I said. "*Congratulations!!*" And I hugged her and we began talking about those things that follow those types of conversations. Gender. Names. Nursery decor. Fluffy fillers to soften the pain that she was carrying so heavily on her shoulders.

Eight months later, I ran into her again at another retreat in another town. She started to cry. And she shared with me her side of the story. Though she was five months pregnant when we met, she told me that I was only the *second* person to congratulate her on her pregnancy. The first? Her doctor. Everyone else? They judged. They worried. They looked down on it all and waved it away as a consequence to a choice and asked what she was going to do.

Our one brief conversation that afternoon allowed for a life-altering transformation in how she viewed her pregnancy. Before, she hated that child. It represented her sin and was the proverbial scarlet letter for all the world to see. And judge. And to worry about. And look down on. For the first time, after those few moments, she wanted to keep her baby. For the first time, she loved that baby.

She told me she, too, had heard our story before she arrived. She knew of our struggle for a family. And if I had said anything else in that moment, things would have ended much differently. If, instead of congratulating her, I had spoken of our desire for a family of our own, or shared my own pain, she told me she would have literally handed him over. Signed on the dotted line of adoption papers without giving it a second thought. But I didn't. Somehow, I had the discernment and the wherewithal to realize it wasn't about me. And God used the woman struggling with a then five year battle with infertility to entirely transform the perspective of a young, ashamed Christian with an unwanted pregnancy.

She went home. She had her baby. And a short time later, she married his daddy.

How easily I could have missed that moment. I could have *messed* that moment. If I had chosen to love on myself and lick my own wounds instead of loving on her, this child's life would have been drastically different. I went into that retreat wanting my pain to be recognized. The day my period started, marking the five year anniversary, I drew the line in the sand. I had enough of hope deferred and decided it was time to set hope aside for awhile. That very same weekend, God started teaching me about thankfulness and joy.

And He graciously showed me a glimpse at the purpose behind the pain.

TREASURES *of* DARKNESS

WEEK 7: THANKFULNESS & JOY

- DAY 1 -

We're starting this week on the heels of studying affliction. And I can't think of a better subject to now focus our attention on than joy. I picked up one of my favorite books this week, and did what any normal person does: flipped to the middle and started reading. It was as if Ann Voskamp was continuing our conversation on affliction with a segue into joy and thanksgiving: *"Holding my head in my hands, I ask it honest before God and children and my daily mess: 'Can we really expect joy all the time?' I know it well after a day smattered with rowdiness and worn a bit ragged with bickering, that I may feel disappointment and the despair may flood high, but to* **give thanks** *is an action and* **rejoice** *is a verb and these are not mere pulsing emotions. While I may not always feel joy, God asks me to give thanks in all things, because He knows that the* ***feeling*** *of joy begins in the* ***action*** *of thanksgiving."*[1]

The hardest part of enduring affliction is counting it all joy. In Acts 5, Peter and the other apostles had been imprisoned for their faith then, very quickly after the Angel of the Lord busted them out, they found themselves on trial. Again. And this time, the council wanted them dead. *"So they departed from the presence of the council, rejoicing that they were counted worthy to suffer shame for His name."* (Acts 5:41)

I remember being in college and sitting at a coffee shop with a good friend discussing all the difficult things that come with being 20. I was lamenting to her about something long since forgotten, but what will never be forgotten is when she stopped, looked me straight in the eyes, and said "Jane, you should actually be really thankful that you're facing this because God sees your heart, and He recognizes something in it that shows Him *you can handle this.*"

Read James 1:2-3 and write the verse here: _____
_____
_____

Counting it all joy denotes a more deliberate and careful judgement - a subjective judgement which has feeling rather than thought for its ground. The very idea of it seems so backwards, because we often don't feel joy in our trials. But, as we already mentioned above, the *feeling* of joy begins in the *action* of the choosing to not despair.

I shared in the introduction to this week about the time that I simply stopped hoping. I stopped hoping for a family. I stopped hoping for a miracle. I stopped hoping for one positive pregnancy test after five dozen negative ones. At the same time I made that dangerous decision, God started pressing on me the habit of thankfulness. Over and over and

---

[1]   Ann Voskamp, One Thousand Gifts: A Dare to Live Fully Right Where You Are (Zondervan, 2010)

over, He was just as persistent with thanksgiving as He has been with the word "breath" throughout this study. I didn't realize the connection then, but it began the very month I drew the line in my heart.

I sat in an empty cafeteria on a grey February morning at a women's retreat. The same women's retreat you read about in the introduction. Though over a hundred women were in attendance, that morning everything was silent. We were instructed to take a vow of silence from the time we got up that morning until breakfast. A time to save our words and our hearts for God alone. To be honest, I sat down that morning wanting to cry and complain to God about the wait. To sit in the unfairness of it all. But He had other plans for me. I happened to read a devotional on my phone that I had never read before. The opening verse was from Genesis 25 - Isaac entreating the Lord for his wife because she was barren. Immediately, through the frustration, I knew that still, after all these years, God *still* hears my cries. In all our affliction, He is afflicted. The very thing we studied last week. Though I've trained myself to put on the happy face and laugh and joke while inside I still feel three steps away from tears, He still sees. He knows. And He hasn't forgotten.

Instead of taking things into his own hands or finding someone else who could give him a child like his parents did, Isaac prayed for his wife. The scripture doesn't show the waiting. However, if you read carefully, there is a 20 year gap compacted into seven verses in Genesis 25. Isaac was forty years old when he married Rebekah. And he was sixty when she finally gave birth to twins. Eventually, in His way...in His time..He answered their prayer.

Then came devotional number two. Read John 11:41 and write it in your journal.

The death of Lazarus - a close friend of Jesus. A man Jesus could have saved before death. But He didn't. He loved. *Therefore He waited.* Re-read the verse you just wrote down. Thanksgiving always precedes the miracle. Jesus is giving thanks for what He is about to receive - a basic truth of prayer taught to us when we're little, but it easily becomes a habit exclusively limited to a meal. As Jesus was about to raise Lazarus from the dead, He was building the faith of the bystanders. The ones watching. Waiting. And He thanked His Father in advance of the miracle. I ended my time that morning with these words:

"Praise is really the most vital preparatory ministry to the working of miracles. Miracles are wrought by spiritual power, and spiritual power is always proportional to our faith."

PRAISE CHANGES THINGS. Nothing so pleases God in connection with our prayer as our praise, and nothing so blesses the man who prays as the praise which he offers. I got a great blessing once in China in this connection. I had received bad and sad news from home, and deep shadows had covered my soul. I prayed, but the darkness did not vanish. I summoned myself to endure, but the darkness only deepened. Just then I went to an inland station and saw on the wall of the mission home these words: 'Try Thanksgiving.' I did, and in a moment every shadow was gone, not to return. Yes, the Psalmist was right, 'It is a good thing to give thanks unto the Lord.'" [2]

Spend some time in thanksgiving prayer to God today. It really does change things, if nothing else but your perspective. And sometimes that's the only thing that needs to be changed.

---

[2] *Streams in the Desert, August 4th*

TREASURES of DARKNESS

WEEK 7: THANKFULNESS & JOY

- DAY 2 -

We left off yesterday with a look into my prayer journal - a time of weary faith and the decision to set aside hope because the disappointment just wasn't worth it anymore. I know at the time I was moving into self-protection mode. Just like the stages of grief, there are stages in waiting on God for a still unanswered prayer. Faith ebbs and flows. Anger comes and goes. But we need to be faithful and persistent to turn it around.

Eight weeks after that women's retreat I told you about yesterday - when God told me very specifically what I needed to do next in this journey - I still hadn't made thankfulness a habit. In fact, I ignored it. My journal was filled with highlighted quotes of sorrow. *When shall my time ever come?*

Read Romans 12:12 and write the verse here: _____
_____
_____

Patience in suffering isn't easy. Spurgeon calls "rejoicing in hope" a warm compress and "patience in tribulation" an ice bath. Both are therapeutic, but one is inherently more difficult to sit through. I was forcing myself to sit through a perpetual ice bath and cutting out the warm compress.

Have you ever found yourself jealous over someone else's list of thankfulness? _____
_____
_____
_____

Eight weeks after getting hit on the head with thankfulness, God was about to bring it to me again. I had been reading a friend's blog[1] - particularly her new tradition of gratitude posted in list form every Friday. As I read through her list, I was jealous. Then I was convicted for being jealous because God had called me to begin a habit of thankfulness weeks prior and I ignored it. And these things were my stumbling block on the road to thankfulness:

I want to be able to fill my list with tales of my children.
I want to have those parenting moments I know I will laugh at later, but aren't so pretty right now.
I want to have the muddy fingerprints on my glass door and the makings of leftover forts strewn about my house.

[1] www.karipatterson.com

I want crumbs on the floor, trinkets tucked into the oddest places, and children's music playing by default in my car. But instead, I'm alone in an empty house for half the time. The only messes I clean up are the ones Josh and I create. I was in the throws of the kind of empty sorrow that comes when hope is set aside. I had been sitting in an ice bath for weeks. And I desperately wanted God to apply the warm compress and fill my heart with gladness so full that there was no longer any room for tears. But I had to *choose* gladness. I had to *choose* thankfulness. I had to *choose* to find the little blessings.

I had to *choose* to start looking at what is and stop staring at what isn't. To see all that He's freely giving me and look past the one thing He's withholding. And I had to choose to say yes to whatever it is He is giving, even if it's the antithesis of every childhood dream. Because making that choice means living a dream I never expected. When He says "no" to my dreams, I need to be thankful that He's saying "yes" to His dreams *for* me (which, incidentally, included moving to Maui). I needed to learn how to count it all joy...even if my way, my dream, or my prayer never ends up happening.

Going back to Genesis, and Eve's choice to eat the apple in the Garden (the immediate repercussions of which we studied last week), we really see the very first sin of all humanity: the sin of ingratitude. *"Our fall was, always has been, and always will be, that we aren't satisfied in God and what He gives."* [2]

God was hammering it in hard, and I was finally ready to listen. In obedience, I began counting my joys instead of my sorrows. Because at some point, the grieving process needs to end.

Spend the rest of your time reading the following verses and turn them into prayers in your journal.

Psalm 95:2-3
Psalm 100 (I love the Amplified version in the latter part of verse 4: " Be thankful *and say so to Him.*")
Psalm 107:21-22 (verse 21 is actually repeated four times in this psalm!)
Psalm 116:17
Ephesians 5:20
Philippians 4:6
1 Thessalonians 5:16-18
Hebrew 13:15

[2] Ann Voskamp, One Thousand Gifts: A Dare to Live Fully Right Where You Are (Zondervan, 2010)

TREASURES of DARKNESS

WEEK 7: THANKFULNESS & JOY

- DAY 3 -

Four months before that women's retreat we began our week with, God and I hashed it out for two hours at my kitchen table on an October morning. Together, we stood at the crossroads of Isaiah 61 and I had to make a choice. The day before I was praying (again) through the continual sadness I just couldn't shake. The sadness that eventually led to my decision to set aside hope. As God pointed out the markers of Isaiah 61, He also pointed to every single thing I was clinging to and He wanted to remove. He stood by ready to remove my headdress of ashes and sackcloth of private grieving and I quickly realized I was at the very backwards (and yet somehow completely normal) place of not wanting to let any of it go. I wanted to hold onto the sadness and grieving because a small part of me believed that as long as I was visibly sorrowful, God would fulfill my prayer sooner.

I feared that choosing joy and gladness meant that I no longer asked for a family. That God would no longer see my need. And that, without my constant reminding, He would forget about it altogether.

Read Genesis 2:18 and write the verse here: _____
_____

Adam was perfectly content in tending and keeping the garden. He never once expressed his need to God for a helper comparable to him. He was simply doing what God told him to do, *but God recognized the need*. So He made Eve. Without Adam ever even having to ask. Read Isaiah 61:1-3. Write a list of every negative thing God wanted to take away from His people: _____
_____
_____
_____
_____
_____

Now make a list of every good thing He wanted to replace them with:
_____
_____
_____
_____
_____
_____

Thankfulness is a choice. Just like walking out of a prison when the doors have been opened is a choice. Allowing ourselves to be comforted is a choice. Trading beauty for ashes is a choice. Replacing mourning with the oil of joy is a choice. And it's not just a one-time end-all kind of choice. These are the kind of choices we need to make over and over again. Which is why I circled back around to this chapter as God was kneading the dough of my faith and pounding the importance of thankfulness into my brain.

As I lay myself out before God, He rubs my raw emotions smooth, pouring His oil of joy on my dry bones of character. Prayer without ceasing is only possible in a life of continual thanks. And the only way to be a woman of prayer is to be a woman of thanks. God, please...teach us how to create a habit of thanksgiving!

Spend the rest of your time today practicing the habit of thankfulness in prayer.

TREASURES *of* DARKNESS

WEEK 7: THANKFULNESS & JOY

- DAY 4 -

I used to dread weekends. For three years of our marriage, Josh worked at least one weekend day thanks to the world of retail. And I hated it. I would spend countless mornings crying at my kitchen table, pouring my heart out in my prayer journal over the silence in our home. But one morning, I spent an hour basking in the silence. No music. No television. No conversation happening or the noise of someone else moving about the house. Just me. My coffee. My favorite blanket. And the few snowflakes falling. I'd started a list of thankfulness in my journal nine months prior when I began reading *One Thousand Gifts* - a list that I've added to here and there over time. That morning, in the silence, I added numbers 251-291. Here are a few of them:

251. Iridescent bubbles in my coffee, creamer swirling joy.
255. Evergreen trees in the dead of winter.
258. Josh's love for books spilling onto our shelf with commentaries at the ready anytime I'm in need.
261. Friday night dance parties.
270. More joy than sorrow these days.
271. More joy than sorrow. That counts for two.
276. Counting it all joy by counting my joys.

I've been thinking a lot about thankfulness and joy over the last couple of days. Joy and thankfulness. Thankfulness brings about the joy. Joy encourages thankfulness. The two cannot be separated.

I've long been intrigued with the idea of the oil of joy, also called the oil of gladness, and finally dug a little bit deeper into it. Charles Spurgeon wrote an entire sermon on the oil of joy alone in 1913, and describes the cultural history at the time: *"Oil was largely used by Orientals upon festive occasions."* (My friend, Hannah, is Korean and cringes anytime anyone refers to her as "oriental". This is where she would interject and assert that she's not a rug! But I digress.) *"The oil which makes man's face to shine was associated with the bread which strengthens man's heart and with the wine which makes glad the heart of man, because these are the chief provisions of a banquet. Before the feast, or during the entertainment, the guests were refreshed with perfumed oil which would either be poured upon the head, or furnished for anointing the face. It was part of a great feast."*

I'm not sure I'd be all that receptive to a host standing by with a bottle of olive oil ready to pour onto my head or smear onto my face upon greeting me at a party. But taken in the context of the time period we're talking about, showers weren't part of a daily practice. The first commercial deodorant wasn't even introduced until the 1800s. People walked everywhere. They were perpetually dirty. And probably quite smelly. Spurgeon goes on to say: *"At feasts, the perfume poured upon the heads of the guests was an appropriate thing. It suited the feast, it made the guests feel at home, and it gave refreshment all around as the delicious perfume sweetened the air."*

I can't help but think again about another Hannah in 1 Samuel 1, and the state that her sorrow left her: in deep anguish - a state that is *always* accompanied by a loss of appetite. I love how there's no grey area with God. There is not a verse anywhere in scripture that says He gives us a spirit of melancholy. He doesn't trade out our mourning for a mediocre in between. He intends for the trade to leave us as it left Hannah:

Write 1 Samuel 1:17-18 here: _____
_____
_____
_____

Read Isaiah 35:10 and write it here: _____
_____
_____
_____

Now read Isaiah 51:11. Sound familiar?

To a hemorrhaging heart whose only outward indication of the turmoil within is a constant stream of tears, He applies the warm compress of His joy - pressing until the tears stop. Because His joy *always* stops the tears. And I'd rather have the oil of joy smeared all over my face than smeared mascara from crying.

Can you think of a time when God met you during a particular time of crying and turned it into supernatural joy? It could be the frustrated tears following a fight with your spouse, or an argument with a family member. It could be the loss of a loved one, or an unanswered prayer. Describe that time here: _____
_____
_____
_____
_____
_____
_____

We're going to end with Psalm 30:5. Read carefully each word of a wonderful promise of hope.

"When the Sun of Righteousness comes, we wipe our eyes, and joy chases out intruding sorrow. Who would not be joyful that knows Jesus? The first beams of the morning bring us comfort when Jesus is the day-dawn." (Charles Spurgeon)

God I pray that You would turn our winter's night into a summer's day. Turn our sighing into singing. Turn our grief into gladness, our mourning into music, our bitter into sweet, and our ashes into beauty...that You may be glorified.

TREASURES *of* DARKNESS

WEEK 7: THANKFULNESS & JOY

- DAY 5 -

I want to begin our last day of this week together looking at one very important piece of Isaiah 61: the very first verse. Read Isaiah 61:1, and then write the first part of the verse here: _____
_____
_____

The introduction to this chapter makes the verses immediately following possible. Without the Spirit of God in our lives, we are bound to a life of perpetual sorrow. Continued disappointment. Because on our own, *we are not able.*

Read Psalm 45:7 and write the verse here: _____
_____
_____

This verse is a working description of God filling Christ with the Spirit. The trinity at work separately. Yet together. It's one of those things that boggles your mind if you think about it for too long. 2 Peter 1:4 says we are partakers of the divine nature. 2 Corinthians 3:18 tells us that we are being transformed into His very own image by the Spirit of God Himself. The same Spirit that anoints Jesus fills us. And we are anointed with the oil of gladness.

The word "anoint" in Psalm 45:7 means to smear or to consecrate; to stroke, to draw the hand over anything.

Read the following verses and then write them in the spaces provided:

Isaiah 25:8 (the first part of the verse) _____
_____

Revelation 7:17 (the last part of the verse) _____
_____

Revelation 21:4 _____
_____

When we allow God to comfort us, and wipe away our tears, He is single-handedly wiping the tears and smearing the oil of joy onto our faces all at once. When a mother comforts her child, whether sick, hurt, or just in need of some cuddling, she strokes the hair. Or rubs the back. Or brushes her fingers across the cheek. God is doing the very same thing to us when we allow Him to comfort us in times of sorrow or mourning. But we have to recognize that He's also anointing us with the Spirit, leaving the visible mark of the oil of gladness, to walk forward in joy.

Read Galatians 5:22 and write it here: _____
_____
_____
_____
_____

There are times when you're filled with the Spirit. And there are times when you're rubbed all over with the oil of the Spirit. All I know is that if you're full of love, joy, peace, patience, kindness, goodness, faithfulness, gentleness, and self-control, there's no room for sorrow, mourning, ashes, heaviness, and strongholds.

Think back to the very first week of our study when we talked about the tongue. You can't bless God and curse a person at the same time. You can't lick your wounds and count your joys at the same time. You can't sit in the dust in sackcloth and run the race with endurance at the same time.

At some point, we need to choose which we're going to go after. And then run after it with all we've got.

I was 19 when I got baptized in a pool on the Oregon State University campus in my jeans and sweatshirt. As I stood in the water, one man was leading a room full of people in worship with his guitar. I'll never forget the song they were singing: *"I'm trading my sorrows, I'm trading my shame, I'm laying them down for the joy of the Lord. I'm trading my sickness, I'm trading my pain, I'm laying them down for the joy of the Lord."*

Spend the rest of your time in prayer in your journal. If you're saying nothing else besides thanking Jesus for the ultimate trade (our sin for His salvation) then it's time well spent.

THIS WEEK'S NUGGET:

*I have set the LORD always before me; Because He is
at my right hand I shall not be moved.
Therefore my heart is glad and my glory rejoices,
my flesh also will rest in hope.*

Psalm 16:8-9

TREASURES *of* DARKNESS

WEEK 8: FAITH & HOPE

- INTRODUCTION -

I'm writing the introduction to this week in the summer of 2014 - nearly three years *after* the homework was written. And I pause, looking for the words. Because I am in a much different place than when I started the homework. Before, I was wrestling with hope and sovereignty and His holy plan. I was going to chemotherapy sessions and waiting for scan results and hoping for miracles and playing cards and living life more intentionally than I ever had before. At some point through my fight, He put my anxiety at ease, calming the type-A frustration begging to know how to do this right. How to navigate these waters. How to be prepared for His end result (whatever it was). How to hope. And what, exactly, to hope for. And then He whispered so simply: *Hope for healing. If I take away the cancer, she will be healed physically. If I take her home, she will be healed spiritually and in a new body. Either way...***I will heal**. So I moved forward in hope, rediscovering my long lost hope for heaven. Because somehow, along the way, it got confused with hope for things in this life. Sadly, I wasn't sure when.

On November 23, 2012, Shawna lost her battle with cancer.

I typed the words, and then I sat there. Frozen. Fingers poised on they keyboard. Unsure of what to write next. Unsure of how to unknot the complicated ball of faith and hope when this one thing that happened ... happened. And it doesn't make sense. Still. *Yet hope remains.* Because when health fails, hope promotes the health of our countenance. When life falls apart and our very souls are disquieted within us, roaring and turbulent, hope is our help. Quieting the disquiet.

When prayers go unanswerd. And tragedy happens. And life cannot be revived. *Hope is the victory.* Hope is the salvation. Hope is the anchor of soul connecting us to the presence of the holiest God hidden inside the holiest of holy places. Hope is our surety. Hope is our steadfast.

Then, I was against all hope believing in hope. Now, I'm hoping to live by sight and not by faith. To talk with God as I talk to a friend. To worship Him in glory and to dance with the angels (one blonde angel in particular).

"Sweet is it that our hope should rest in Him Who is never shaken; should abide in Him Who never changeth; should bind us to Him who can hold us fast to Himself, Who Alone is the full contentment of the soul; should, as it were, enter into Him; since 'in Him is our being', Who is Love. Sweeter yet is it, that this is our hope is no fruit of our own thought. We do not come at it by our understandings; we do not gather it for ourselves even from His Word alone. It is, with Faith and Love, His Gift, poured out within us, drawing us upward to Himself. Yet Holy Scripture has yet one sweeter word still. Not only is our hope IN Him, but He Himself IS our Hope." [1]

---

[1] Edward Bouverie Pusey, *Parochial Sermons* (Oxford, 1853), *pg. 38*

TREASURES *of* DARKNESS

WEEK 8: FAITH & HOPE

- DAY 1 -

Confession: I put off writing this week. As in I wrote this on a Saturday when I should have four days of homework written already but I had barely finished one. I'd known throughout my procrastination that this week would be focused on hope. And I also knew that hope is the one thing I struggle with the most. I'd vacillated on it more than anything else in my spiritual walk through these significantly difficult years. And, because of that, I wanted to approach this week in full conviction that I have learned, or am learning, what I'm teaching. That I believe it. And cling to it.

I also knew that half of the homework was already written out in the pages of my prayer journal - things I've already wrestled through privately with God. While it was tempting to simply find the pages and regurgitate it, I knew I needed to re-study it. Because I felt that familiar frustration niggling in my brain that leads to disappointment. Which leads to setting hope on a shelf in self-protection. So I procrastinated. And prayed. And added another dozen items to my joys counted out. Reminding myself that thankfulness and joy encourage faith and hope.

Go to Psalm 16:8-9. Read it, then write the words here: _____

_____
_____
_____
_____
_____

Last week we studied joy and thankfulness. This week we're beginning to study hope by first looking at joy. Because hope always starts with joy. Gladness. Rejoicing. A cheerful countenance. Loud expressions of joy as those who make merry with wine. The I-can't-contain-it kind of joy. The I-can't-help-but-dance kind of joy. That's what the words are referring to in verse eight.

And then comes hope. But not just having hope. *Resting* in hope. Settling into it. Lying down. Abiding. In hope.

I found it really interesting that hope, in this particular verse, means security. Safety. Confidence. That word "security" was especially interesting to me after realizing in the summer of 2010 that my struggle to wait for a family had become an insecurity. The fear of the not having had eclipsed the hope and faith of the waiting.

I thought again of the verses we studying in Isaiah 61 last week, and added one more item to the list of verse three for my own personal reminder. Beauty for ashes. The oil of joy for mourning. The garment of praise for the spirit of heaviness. *Hope for insecurity and fear.*

My biggest fear in this season of waiting is never having a family of my own and, with that, not having a legacy.

What is your biggest fear either overall or in this particular season of life? _____
_____
_____
_____

The word used for hope in Psalm 16:9 literally means to dwell without fear. Choosing hope means staring your fears in the face and not letting them debilitate you any longer.

Read 2 Timothy 1:7 and write it in your journal.

The Greek word for "spirit" has quite a hefty list of definitions. Fifth down in the list caught my eye and provided the trail marker for this week. I bet you can guess what it is. *Breath* - of nostrils or mouth. God breathed life into us, giving us His very breath in Genesis. By His breath we either bless or curse men. By His breath we either hope or fear. It's our choice how we use it. But He did not give us His breath for the expression of fear. He gave it to us for the power of performing miracles - and sometimes that power is exerted in the mere waiting in expectation of them. He gave us His breath as a sound mind. Not an irrational one. He did *not* give us a spirit of fear, yet it's so easy to slip into a habit of it.

We're going to end our time reading 1 John 4:18. Read the verse and write it here: _____
_____
_____
_____

As I was studying the verse, I got a bur in my spur (or the breath of God whispering in my ear) to head over to wikipedia and look up the word fear. What I found was an interesting tidbit of modern information that perfectly complements what John wrote over 2,000 years ago: *"Scientists from Zurich studies show that the hormone oxytocin related to stress and sex reduces activity in your brain fear center (the amygdala)."* When I looked more into oxytocin, I found this: *"Recent studies have begun to investigate oxytocin's role in various behaviors, including social recognition, pair bonding (a strong affinity that develops in some species between the males and females), anxiety, and maternal behaviors. For this reason, it is sometimes referred to as the **love hormone**".* The wikipedia entry goes on to say: *"Many studies have shown a correlation of oxytocin with human bonding, increases in trust, and **decreases in fear**."*

In 95 AD, John introduced the idea that love casts out fear. And today, there are scientific studies to prove it.

*Oh LORD...when fear begins to creep into my heart and steal my joy because the wait for an unanswered prayer turns into years, help me to remember that You **love** me. With Lazarus, Mary and Martha, You loved. **Therefore** you waited. Help me to recognize that, remember it, and allow Your perfect love to cast out my fear.*

TREASURES *of* DARKNESS

WEEK 8: FAITH & HOPE

- DAY 2 -

One morning, in late 2010, I sat at my usual perch at the kitchen table: prayer journal and Bible open, pen ready, fresh coffee in my favorite mug. These are the words I wrote:

It's interesting how this year has been a circle of hope, discouragement, thankfulness, hope again, fear of hoping, thankfulness... it's an exercise in endurance. But still, so often, my type-A personality comes out. I panic because I need to know the right thing to hope for. We get excited to adopt and plan to start budgeting for it. But then I get convicted about miracles. I know adoption is amazing across the board...but, LORD, is our decision to adopt directly related to our faith (or lack of it)?

Then I wrote out my fears. The first one I talked about yesterday. The second one has to do with faith:

I fear not believing You. That my lack of faith will directly impact everything else in my life.

My biggest conviction throughout this entire season has consistently been that, if I'm ever gifted with pregnancy, I want to be caught in the act of believing. I want to be found on the upswing. When I wrestle with hope, discouragement, thankfulness, and sorrow, I want to always come out on top with faith. I want to actively gather the treasures of darkness and not just sit in the darkness wringing my hands. I don't want to be caught off-guard in unbelief and discouragement.

Two weeks after I wrote the prayer above, I studied a verse in Job. Read Job 7:6 and write it here:

_____

_____

Matthew Henry said this about Job's words: "My time is now but short, and there are but a few sands more in my glass, which will speedily run out... Job was without hope of being restored to his former prosperity...our days are like a weaver's shuttle, thrown from one side of the web to the other in the twinkling of an eye; and then back again, to and fro, until at length it is quite exhausted of the thread it carried, and then we are cut off, like a weaver, our life...while we are living, as we are sowing, we are weaving. Every day like the shuttle leaves a thread behind it. Many weave the spider's web, which will fail them. If we are weaving to ourselves holy garments and robes of righteousness, we shall have the benefit of them when our work comes to be received and every man shall reap as he sowed and wear as he wove."

I initially wrote the verse in Job down because I was intrigued by the part about days spent without hope. But my time that morning took a completely different turn. While Matthew Henry doesn't outrightly mention hope, his words encourage it. We *have* to hope - it's the thing that propels us when everything else is dismal. Hope keeps the weaver's shuttle moving. Consistently. Tightly. Strongly. Providing a garment without holes that will last. A garment that the next generation will use. And it's my prayer that, through this season, my faith and the words found in my journals for generations after me to read will be well-woven.

Then I began to think about the robes of righteousness. Go back to Isaiah 61, read verse 10 and write it here:
_____
_____
_____
_____

We are promised robes of righteousness from God Himself. Revelation even speaks of every nation, tribe, people, and tongue clothed in white robes. Then there are the Levitical priests we studied in week two. They had their own clothes that were worn in the day-to-day duties. But they changed their clothes before entering the temple. And I began to think.

Some day, when we stand before God and our faith has become sight, what if the garments we wear are based on the way we wove the thread of our lives? The idea forces us to live life premeditatedly. Intentionally. If we imagine the spiritual garments we are presented to God in as ones which we weave ourselves, and which God replaces with His robes of righteousness in the end, we'd react more carefully. We'd ensure to loosen that knot in our faith that's beginning to form or that snag in our joy. We'd remove the obstacles that threaten to leave holes.

I absolutely know the need for grace. And I'm certainly not saying that the robes of righteousness promised to us are based on our works. But what if we took a little bit of ownership in trying to make our spiritual garments as beautiful and spotless as possible? In this life, we are presented with one spool of thread and one weave. If you can indulge me in this thought, how are your spiritual garments currently looking? _____
_____
_____
_____

Spend the rest of your time in your journal this morning. *God may we weave beautiful garments of faith. Show us where our thread might be knotted and then help us to get it straightened out again.*

TREASURES *of* DARKNESS

WEEK 8: FAITH & HOPE

- DAY 3 -

So far, this week, we've talked about fear. We've discussed how hope can provide the clothing pattern for the very robes we will stand before God in some day. Today I want to talk about the honest struggle that I find with hope. The questions I've asked God, and where He's pointed me in scripture.

Two weeks after Shawna was diagnosed with stage four colon cancer, I sat at my kitchen table on a quiet Saturday morning. I was reading a book by Chuck Swindoll called "Laugh Again Hope Again: Two Books to Inspire a Joy-Filled Life". And I began writing in my journal:

"When life hurts and dreams fade, nothing helps like hope." "Hope requires expectation." That's what I've been struggling with this week. LORD, what should I be expecting? I've learned enough about Your sovereignty in the last year to know that it can overshadow any expectation I might have. *"Hope must be expectation without parameters."* Hope for a family without my time line attached to it. Hope for healing without my definition of what that includes.

"Take away our hope, and our world is reduced to something between depression and despair," Swindoll says just three pages into the book. Despair is the opposite of hope - a sin in the eyes of the Catholic church because it shows a loss of faith. And I found myself in a crisis of belief because I felt absolutely helpless against the sovereignty of God.

I read my journals and I see the tug of war on the pages. The desperate journey to understand hope and faith. The search for the faith to believe that His word is right. Straightforward. Pleasing. Truth. All His work is done in truth, which is also translated *faithfulness*. My mind swims with how it's all connected. Affliction. Joy. Thankfulness. Hope. Faithfulness. Truth. Belief. I had you read the last part of Lamentations 3 in week six's homework. Today, you will read the first part. It perfectly illustrates the very struggle I found myself in - one prophet's agony, and the never-ending compassion of an ever-loving God. The first 17 verses describe the anguish and suffering in pure, raw emotions to God. And then we get to verse 18. Read verses 1-18, and write verse 18 here: _____

_____

While I personally never said out loud that my hope had perished, I quietly believed it. I love the cross-reference for this verse: Psalm 31:22. Read it and write it here: _____

_____

_____

Even when I hastily, wrongfully drew a line in the sand that I determined to never cross again, He still remained faithful. Even though I stopped hoping, He never stopped listening. He never once took His eyes off of me. The word "perished" used in Lamentations 3:18 means literally lost. To lose oneself. To wander - especially used of a lost and wandering sheep that disappears in the desert. Flip over to Luke 15 and read verses three through six.

He watches us beginning to wander. And He will bring us back, just like He did with the prophet in Lamentations. Just like He has done with me. Go back to Lamentations 3 and read verses 19-21. In just a matter of verses, the prophet moves from perished hope to having hope. Adam Clarke, a British theologian, wrote these words based on this section of scripture in the late 1700s: *"The Sovereign God **alone** can revive (hope)."*

Lost hope comes as a result of disappointed expectations. And when my expectation of God is reduced to nothing, I am basically saying *"I'm disappointed in You. I can't trust You. I have no confidence in You."* Oh God, forgive me for ever getting to that place! The irony is we set aside hope because we feel like we can't trust God, whether or not the words are actually spoken, and yet He is the only one that can revive it within us again. Adam Clarke continues by saying *"Hope is essentially necessary to faith; he that hopes can't not believe; if there be no expectation, there can be no confidence... Hope cannot live if there be no exercise. If hope become impatient, faith will be impossible."*

Read Lamentations 3:22-29, then write verses 22-23 here: _____
_____
_____

"Things might be bad, but they also could be worse. Therefore, there is hope that they may be better." (Matthew Henry)

For nine months, God had been training me. Understanding sovereignty and providence. Recognizing the place for suffering and affliction in life. Waiting on Him. The power of raw, believing prayer. Looking for the treasures - the same way I wait in expectation for the word "breath" to show up every single week throughout this study. Laughing. Crying. And laughing again. Trading my sorrows for His oil of gladness. Remembering that even though He says no, He is still a beautiful, and good, and just God. Which promotes thankfulness. And I circle back around again to hope. And I lift my hands to believe again.

Great is His faithfulness. Morning by morning, new mercies I see - if I train my eyes to look for them. And if His faithfulness is so great, how can I possibly begin to even think of setting aside my hope? Or turn my back from believing Him. Why? Because my faith is tired?

Read Psalm 145:17 and write the verse here: _____
_____
_____

The KJV translates it this way: "The LORD is righteous in all His ways, and holy in all His works." All of His works are holy. Good and bad. Cancer. Infertility. Health. Illness. Death. Life. Poverty. Provision. He is holy in *all of it*. And when we don't understand any of it, He gives strength for today and bright hope for tomorrow. Because His faithfulness is great. *God...may we never, ever forget that.*

TREASURES of DARKNESS

WEEK 8: FAITH & HOPE

- DAY 4 -

This week, we're exploring hope in the very time line that I studied it. And this morning finds us in June 2011, one week after yesterday's words were written. I was doing a study on faithfulness when God pointed me right where He wanted me. I was instructed to read Hebrews 11:1 and read verse 11 by mistake. Read the verse and write it here:

_____
_____
_____

"The same things that are the object of our hope are the object of our faith." (Matthew Henry) Faith says that Jesus is the Messiah and will come back. Hope says that He will come back in our lifetime.

As I began exploring more verses on hope, I realized a pattern - hoping *on* God. Hoping *in* Christ. Hoping *in* salvation. That's the intention for hope. Yet, just like everything else, we try to make it about ourselves. At this very moment, what is one specific thing you're hoping for? _____
_____
_____

This is where the rubber meets the road: Are you simply hoping for that thing, or are you hoping that God will glorify Himself through you *using* that thing? Or, do you hope that He will glorify Himself through the wait of it? Self is the tangle. It always has been, and it always will be. I was so convicted that I hoped more for this thing on my life list than I did for heaven. If a family was the object of my hope...what does that say about my faith?

1 John 3:3 says "Everyone who has this hope in Him purifies himself, just as He is pure." Easton's Bible Dictionary defines hope in this verse as opposed to seeing or possessing. The expression "hope *in* Him" ought rather to be, as in the Revised Version "hope *on* Him." In other words, a hope based on God alone.

One of the things I ask Josh to do quite often is love on me. When I say it, he'll give me a quick *"I love you"* and go back to whatever it was he was doing, inevitably followed by me saying *"that's not what I meant."* When I ask my husband to love *on* me, I don't want it to be from afar. And I don't want it to be quick. I mean close interaction. Undivided attention. Holding me. Cuddling with me. Paying attention to me. As I read the definition from above, I tried to imagine if I applied that kind of attention to hope. And I realized that the act of hoping is a much more intimate expression with God. It requires close contact. Consistent conversation. My eyes locked on His. Because He *is* my hope. And I *am* the apple of His eye.

Read Hebrews 6:17-20.

Hope anchors our souls, tethering us to Christ. We just don't know how long that chain is. It could be hundreds of miles. It could be a hundred yards. But we can be certain that the *"interim is an opportunity to develop faith. Because hope is simply faith directed toward the future, and no sharp distinction between faith and hope is attainable. The postponement of the full attainment, through developing faith, gives steadfastness which could be gained in no other way. On the other hand, this steadfastness, produced by hope, reacts again on hope and increases it."* (Matthew Henry)

Does your brain hurt? That's about the time that I throw up my hands and pray that God would simply teach me how to hope. But it's important to recognize the very important spiral effect we've been discussing these last two weeks.

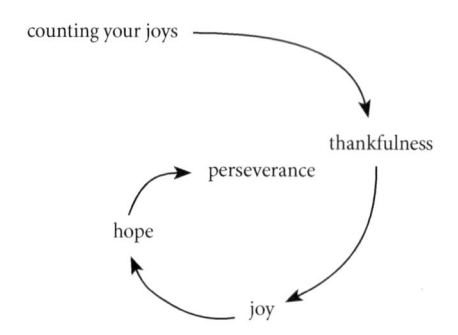

counting your joys → thankfulness → joy → hope → perseverance

I don't know about you, but I'd much rather be tied up in that spiral than one of resentment, bitterness, anger, tears, and sorrow. Those things lead to isolation. They lead to closing a Facebook account because of the abundance of engagement announcements that you just can't take anymore. They lead to avoiding baby showers, and church on baby dedication Sundays. The lead to leaving a church or moving to a different town because of hurt feelings. They lead to putting your wall up and refusing to let anyone close because you've been burned. I want to end today with an interesting translation I found for hope - one of 14 different Hebrew words used in the Old Testament for it: *miqveh*. In addition to expectation and confidence, it also means a congregation, gathering together.

Read Matthew 18:20 and write it here: _____
_____
_____

There is strength in numbers because our hope is Christ. And when we gather together with other believers, our hope is there. Among us. Finally, read Psalm 31:24 and write the verse here: _____
_____
_____

So begins another spiral. When my heart is weak, I must hope on God by hoping in Christ. And when I hope in Christ, He strengthens my heart. Until He pulls my anchor in and my faith is as sight. And there is no more need of hope. *God, thank You that You are my hope. Teach me how to hope **on** You and not in a thing that You are using to pull me closer to You. And above all, I pray that my hope for heaven would eclipse all other things. Be my hope today.*

TREASURES *of* DARKNESS

WEEK 8: FAITH & HOPE

- DAY 5 -

June 8, 2011 - (8:45 am) Wednesday

Thank You Lord that with You there is hope. Hope in the darkness to push through to the end of the tunnel from which the light isn't visible. There is hope when I talk to another girlfriend about cancer in her milk duct and an impending lumpectomy with two rounds of chemo. There is hope when Shawna's brother-in-law goes into the hospital after five days of headaches and they find a grade four brain tumor. There is hope when her cousin has a piece of her back taken out to catch melanoma. There is hope when cancer, like Satan incarnate, seems to be taking over the world. There. Is. Hope.

Without it, prognosis is simply a sand of time tied as a noose around your neck. Depression is the spoon that feeds the darkness. And a person shrivels up. **I have to hope.** *"Solid, stable, sure hope. Hope to press on. Hope to endure. Hope to stay focused. Hope to see new dreams fulfilled." (Hope Again).*

Read 1 Peter 1:3 and write every comforting word here: _____

_____

_____

_____

The KJV uses the words "a lively hope" - *zaō elpis*. To live. *Breathe.* Be among the living. To enjoy real life in the active, blessed kingdom of God with a joyful and confident expectation of eternal salvation. Yes, we can hope for miracles. And we can hope for very specific things that pertain to life. But our hope must remain in Christ.

Two days later, I received an email that brought me to tears from an old friend regarding Shawna's battle with cancer. As a nurse, she shared how difficult it was for her to look at the diagnosis and hope for a miracle. *"Why do Christians so often pray for a miracle of healing?"* she asked. But when I thought of the God we serve, the only determination I could come up with is: *how can we expect anything less?*

Scripture is full of stories that fuel hope. Abraham. Job. Hebrews 11 is full of stories of faith. Men who "against all hope in hope believed." (Romans 4:18) I began to realize as I looked over the names that the people whose suffering and affliction landed them in the Hall of Faith were, for the most part, alone. They didn't have friends surrounding them that were full of faith. Job even had his closest friends condemning him for weeks! It was the faith of lonely men that pushed those around them to believe after the fact. And it is their faith now, thousands of years later, that pushes us to hope. Others can't hope for us, because nobody else knows the struggle we're facing like we do.

I determined in my heart to not let that email sway me. I determined to press on and continue to believe God for a miracle. Nobody can believe on our behalf. It's up to us to believe for ourselves. And to have a living hope. So that someday someone can say about us *"by faith Jane..."*.

Jump ahead in 1 Peter 1 to verse 13, and write it here: _____
_____
_____
_____

Gird up the loins of your mind - a metaphor derived from the practice of the Asians who, in order to be unimpeded in their movements were accustomed to bind their long flowing garments closely around their bodies and fastened them with a leather belt when starting a journey or engaging in any work.

Be calm and collected in your spirit.

And hope to the end - because His mercy is given in proportion to our waiting and hoping for Him (Psalm 33:22) *"Not according to any merit of ours, but according to the measure of grace, of the grace of hope which God had bestowed on us, and encouraged us to exercise on Him in expectation of finding grace and mercy with Him." (John Gill).*

Below is a list of verses throughout the Psalms on hope. Read them. Pray through them. Come back to them as you need to - they are the chain links in our hope anchors.

Psalm 16:9
Psalm 31:24
Psalm 33:18, 22
Psalm 38:15
Psalm 39:7
Psalm 42:5, 11
Psalm 43:5
Psalm 71:5, 14
Psalm 119: 116
Psalm 146:5

THIS WEEK'S NUGGET:

*Then Job answered the LORD and said:
I know that You can do everything, and that
no purpose of Yours can be withheld from You.*

Job 42:1

TREASURES *of* DARKNESS

WEEK 9: SOVEREIGNTY

- INTRODUCTION -

November, 2013 marked the 50th anniversary of the John F. Kennedy assassination. With that came an onslaught of people remembering. Vividly picturing where they were. What they were doing. And how life was forever changed. We were locked into a show on National Geographic that created a meticulous recapping of the event. With play-by-play commentary. *"Fifty years later,"* they narrator said, *"we're still searching for answers."*

In the midst of navigating November, preparing for the anniversary of Shawna's death, and remembering the life-altering event that had taken place just one year earlier, I watched as men and women, alongside the parade route an entire lifetime ago, were still overcome by emotion in telling the story. Five decades later. It's somehow encouraging to know that the emotion will always be there. Yet I have a record player inside my head with the same four words on a constant turntable: *don't get stuck there.*

My alarm went off today and my eyes were greeted by the grey fog of an early fall morning in Oregon. Near freezing with the window open, I cuddled down warm into the down blanket and husband heat, silencing the chime for another six minutes. Soon, responsibility outweighed comfort. With the fireplace on, my favorite sweater wrapped tight, and coffee steaming, I began to read.

"Those who sat in darkness and in the shadow of death, bound in affliction and irons… they fell down, and there was none to help." (Psalm 107:10, 12b)

The words were just a piece of a story. An early morning eavesdropping on a conversation in which one man is giving thanks to the only LORD for His great works of deliverance. *"That's it,"* I thought. *"They're sitting there. In the shadow of death. I want to walk through the shadow of death when my life journey requires it. But LORD, please don't let me get comfortable and dwell here."* I don't want to pick out the curtains and draw up the floorplans for this new type of sorrowful normal. I want to print an amazing photograph and hang it on the wall of a joyful home where I will walk by it daily. And remember. But I want to live in the joy. Not in the frame. Because when I live in the frame, I get stuck on this one gut-wrenching thing: *Unanswered prayer.*

I want to believe. To hope. And not sit in the shadow of death, in the sadness of what He chose not to do, and the jaded cynicism of hope deferred.

At the same time the National Geographic documentary was on, I was working on a personal project that required a login to Shawna's blog for the first time in nearly a year. I came across this post, and am re-writing it here as a reminder to myself that nothing is impossible for Him.

Thursday, May 19, 2011 11:22 am (seven days after her diagnosis)

I sat down a Starbucks table – the same Starbucks where God and I wore out my Bible together a lifetime ago through endless hours studying, praying, and journaling. I sat, and I stared at my journal. Discouraged. Disheartened. Feeling the weight of the world on my shoulders, and then feeling guilty because I wasn't even the one carrying this disease. My brain didn't want to rejoice. My brain didn't want to count the gifts in this season. My brain didn't want to worship. But my heart kept repeating that single line.

"Nothing is impossible for You."

As I opened my Bible and began to read, the verses came tumbling to me. And my pen couldn't keep up quickly enough.

This…this new normal that makes us feel like a leaf tossed about by the hurricane winds of Your sovereignty this new reality that makes hearts across many miles hurt so badly that it's difficult to breathe…this new normal that saps strength, drains emotions, and makes even the strongest in their faith scream at You…this is not impossible for You. This isn't beyond Your power. It's not difficult for You. For You, God, healing is as easy as taking a photograph is for me. It's second nature…no…it's really just Your nature.

You are a God of boundless, bottomless mercy. When human skill and power are quite nonplussed, with You are strength and wisdom sufficient to master the problem. All the powers of men are derived from You. All the actions and directions of the doctors are governed by **You***. (Matthew Henry)*

Thank you, Jesus, for **promising** *that the things which are impossible with men are possible with God. Is anything too hard for the LORD? Ah, LORD God! Behold, You have made the heavens and the earth by Your great power and outstretched arm. There is* **nothing** *too hard for You. You even say Yourself "Behold, I am the LORD, the God of all flesh. Is there anything too hard for Me?" (Luke 18:27, Jer. 32:17, 17)*

You are the God Who parted the sea for Moses and separated the river for Joshua.
You are the God Who made a staff grow blossoms and made a stagnant pond sweet.
You are the God Who fell a 45 foot high, 6 foot thick fortified wall with the shout of an army.
You are the God Who danced with three men in the furnace, untouched by the flames.
You shut the mouths of lions, open the mouths of donkeys, and bring symbols of hope in the mouths of doves.
You turn water into wine and cast demons into swine.
You make the lame walk, the mute talk, the blind see, and leprosy flee.
You raise men from the dead.
You cure the incurable.

You forgive sin.

Nothing is impossible for You.

TREASURES *of* DARKNESS

WEEK 9: SOVEREIGNTY

- DAY 1 -

I'm beginning this week with the same confession I made at the start of last week's homework: I put off writing this section of homework for weeks. We'd had a break and, to be honest, the break was a welcome one for me. But as that break ended, I was at a loss of what to say. Where to start. How to teach on this idea of sovereignty that I too often feel like I'm butting my head against.

I found it interesting when I began to study and discovered that the words "sovereign" and "sovereignty" aren't found in the KJV of scripture. Nor in the NKJV. You do see the word in the New Living Translation, New International Version, English Standard Version, as well as some others, but if you study the original Hebrew words in the verses listed, the word "sovereign" is not included in any of the definitions. Anywhere.

I discovered in my research that the word sovereign was introduced into the English language by the French-speaking sovereigns who governed England in the 12th century. It was originally a French word and was used almost exclusively to describe a mortal, political leader. The word is said to have been introduced into theology by John Calvin - a Frenchman encapsulating his French training for the priesthood, his denial of free will, and his teachings merging church and state. Knowing this, it makes sense that the word "sovereign" is included in the NIV since it wasn't written until 1965.

However, that doesn't negate the doctrine of sovereignty in scripture. It merely gives a title to the theme. In just a short phrase, how would you define the word sovereign? _____

_____

_____

_____

When we speak about the sovereignty of God, we talk about His supremacy. His kingship. His godhood. Saying that God is sovereign is saying that God *is* God. Take a few moments to look up the following verses and write them below:

Daniel 4:35 _____

_____

_____

_____

Psalm 22:28 _____

_____

Psalm 115:3 _____
_____

1 Timothy 6:15-16 _____
_____

"When we say that God is sovereign, we affirm His right to govern the universe, which He has made for His own glory, just as He pleases. We affirm that His right is the right of true Potter over the clay, i.e. that He may mold that clay into whatsoever form He chooses, fashioning out of the same lump one for honor and one for dishonor. We affirm that He is under no rule or law outside of His own will and nature. That God is a law unto Himself, and that He is under no obligation to give an account of His matters to any." [1]

God is under no obligation to explain Himself - a truth particularly hard to swallow when all we want to know is *"why?"* When I stare too long at the unanswered *"why?"*, it becomes my stumbling block. For so long, I've felt like the sovereignty of God was a slow-moving cement wall against which I was helpless to fight. I simply had to allow it to push me along. But it's the continual seeking of answers to questions that He isn't obligated to answer that pushes me against the wall. When I ask Him *"why?"*, I'm essentially turning around and pointing at the thing in question. That suffering. That unanswered prayer. That heartache. *"Why that? Why now?!"*

To some, He delivers. And to some He does not. Read John 5: 1-9.

Jesus approached Bethesda and the pool by the Sheep Gate where there "lay a great multitude of sick people, blind, lame, and paralyzed." He could have chosen to heal every single one of those people if He wanted to. But instead He chose to heal one. And that one man didn't even ask Jesus to be healed. I can all but guarantee it wasn't for lack of faith. The sick man had an infirmity for thirty-eight years. With afflictions that last into years, and even decades, there's a time of asking for healing. And then there's a time where you simply wait for healing because you're all talked out. I'm sure that man had asked God to be healed countless times before this moment. There isn't anything in this section of scripture to support it, but I get the feeling that he was simply resting as he waited. Almost as if he's at peace with the fact that he had this infirmity, there was no one to physically lift him into the healing pool at the appointed time, so he simply laid there and waited.

Read Psalm 37:7 and write the first part of the verse here: _____
_____

When things don't make sense, and prayers go unanswered, I need to rest in the LORD - even if I find myself still waiting and hoping for the same thing thirty-eight years later. Either He will provide the answer for it, or He won't. But He still is God. And I just need to rest in that. What do you need to rest on God with today? Spend the rest of your time setting those things aside and resting fully on Him.

[1] Arthur W. Pink, *Sovereignty of God* (Lightning Source, Inc., 2002) pg. 25

TREASURES OF DARKNESS

TREASURES of DARKNESS

WEEK 9: SOVEREIGNTY

- DAY 2 -

We're going to spend a good chunk of our time today studying Psalm 37:7. Re-write the first part of the verse here:
_____
_____

Now go to blueletterbible.org on your computer, and search for Psalm 37:7. We'll be studying the first part of the verse today, and the second part tomorrow.

Just like we've done throughout the study, look up the Hebrew word for "rest", taking note of the parsing, and write the definition here: _____
_____

Do you remember last week when we were studying Lamentations 3? This same Hebrew word is also used in Lamentations 3:28. So much of our faith requires us to be silent before God. Faith wouldn't be faith if we weren't believing Him for big things. Difficult things. Miraculous things. And part of faith is being silent. Not answering back. Not asking the Potter *"why have you made me this way?"*. Further reading of the definition explains the word "rest" as "hearing someone without speaking". Does this take you back to the exercise I had you do during the week on marriage - asking your husband a question without answering him back or defending yourself? It's the same way with our relationship with Christ. When we answer back, we're defending ourselves - providing an argument as to why we deserve this or don't deserve that. But part of resting is hearing Him without speaking. Even if He's remaining silent on the issue. We need to learn how to be silent before Jehovah while patiently, and with confidence, expecting His aid.

I believe this is exactly where the man was that we looked at yesterday. After thirty-eight years of the same infirmity, He had finally learned to be silent and wait confidently in the aid of God. And, after decades of waiting, Jesus came and healed him without his even having to ask.

If you read Matthew Henry's commentary on this verse, he talks about how we are very quick to busy our minds with our own discontentment and mistrust. That niggling thought in the back of our brain that says "I believe God for this.... But what if...." He reminds us that it is absolutely necessary to arm ourselves against that habit by believing in God. No ifs, ands, or buts. To be reconciled to all He does and acquiesce ourselves in it. Sound familiar? It's the same thing we studied in week five - creating a habit of contentment. When I beat my head against the wall of His sovereignty, I'm working against that habit of contentment.

Though we may not know how, we still need to rest in the fact that He will still make it all work for good to us.

Read Psalm 62:5 and write the verse here: _____
_____

In Psalm 61 (as well as Psalm 62), David was a fugitive. His throne had been occupied by someone else, and he was in constant danger of being killed. (For a real backdrop of exactly what he was dealing with, read 2 Samuel 15-17.) Yet through it all, his conviction was to silently wait for God, *and to silently wait for Him alone* (Psalm 62:1, 5). He confidently waited in silent expectation of divine aid. Quietly hoping and believing three simple yet hard-to-believe things: God had heard him, God had given him a great heritage, and God would protect him.

Because of my own personal experiences, I tend to resonate deeply with extreme examples. The man who had been sick for thirty-eight years speaks to me because suddenly my right-now-wait of eight years for a family isn't so long. David's continual life on the run in legitimate mortal danger convicts me because we see his heart literally poured out in the psalms, seeking God's face every second. Tough circumstances don't always have to be that extreme. But they can still be just as hard.

What is the one thing you're resisting God on today? What is fueling the anxiety? What is making you worry?
_____
_____
_____
_____
_____

There are five things that I know I can believe God for in any circumstance, three of which we covered above:
- God has heard me (Psalm 31:22)
- God has given me a great heritage (Psalm 16:6)
- God will protect me (Psalm 3:3)
- God will defend me (Psalm 18)
- God will glorify Himself through me (Isaiah 43:1-7)

Which one of those most resounds with you today? Spend the rest of your time turning the scripture associated with it into a personal prayer to the Lord.

TREASURES *of* DARKNESS

WEEK 9: SOVEREIGNTY

- DAY 3 -

John Piper, a Minnesota pastor and founder of the Desiring God ministry, has a lifelong passion to *"see and savor the supremacy of God in everything."* When I first read that statement, I began to think about the difference between God's sovereignty and His supremacy. In reality, there isn't a lot of difference between the two. But they do seem to offer very different facets of God's character. While I sometimes feel helpless against His sovereignty, I can *always* stand in awe of His supremacy.

Earlier this week, I referred to the sovereignty of God as a slow-moving concrete wall. It's a picture I can't get out of my head. When I think of sovereignty, it's always paired with that visual representation. Tragedies happen, but life never stops. As I step back further and look at the larger picture (instead of staring at the details until I go cross-eyed), I see that this slow-moving wall is a lifelong time line. I have numbered days. And God has meticulously planned how those days play out. His sovereignty is in the fulfillment of those events. My faith is in the reaction to them. Do I still worship His supremacy in everything at all times?

A very successful lawyer by the name of Haratio Spafford called Chicago home in the late 1800s. He was a man who would become well-acquainted with tribulation, beginning with the death of his only son in 1871 at the age of four. Later that same year, the great Chicago fire destroyed nearly every real estate investment he had. Two years later, in 1873, he and his family planned a trip to Europe. While in Great Britain, he planned to help his good friend Dwight L. Moody and Ira Sankey, whom he had financially supported, with their evangelistic tour. Finishing up last minute business in Chicago, Spafford sent his wife and four girls—ages 11, 9, 7 and 2—ahead of him. On November 22, the S.S. Ville Du Havre struck another ship and sank within twelve minutes, taking the lives of his four daughters with it. Mrs. Spafford cabled her husband *"Saved alone."*

As Spafford crossed the ocean alone to meet his wife, he was notified that they were near the location where the ship went down. It's said that in that very location, Spafford sat on the ship, and wrote these words:

When peace like a river, attendeth my way,
When sorrows like sea billows roll;
Whatever my lot, Thou hast taught me to say,
It is well, it is well, with my soul.
It is well, with my soul, It is well, with my soul,
It is well, it is well, with my soul.
Though Satan should buffet, though trials should come,

Let this blest assurance control,
That Christ has regarded my helpless estate,
And hath shed His own blood for my soul.
My sin, oh, the bliss of this glorious thought!
My sin, not in part but the whole,
Is nailed to the cross, and I bear it no more,
Praise the Lord, praise the Lord, O my soul!
For me, be it Christ, be it Christ hence to live:
If Jordan above me shall roll,
No pang shall be mine, for in death as in life,
Thou wilt whisper Thy peace to my soul.
But Lord, 'tis for Thee, for Thy coming we wait,
The sky, not the grave, is our goal;
Oh, trump of the angel! Oh, voice of the Lord!
Blessed hope, blessed rest of my soul.
And Lord, haste the day when my faith shall be sight,
The clouds be rolled back as a scroll;
The trump shall resound, and the Lord shall descend,
Even so, it is well with my soul.

A man tragically lost all five of his children in just two short years...but he still chose to see the supremacy of God in it all. And his raw, emotional, and deeply personal words to God still provides comfort to countless people today.

I was teaching at a conference in the weeks before Shawna went into hospice when the worship team led 150 women in that song. I couldn't sing it. As hard as I tried, I couldn't choke out the words. That night, as I lay on the cold tile of the bathroom floor weeping all over again, I cried out in honesty and truth and sputtered breaths: *It is* **not** *well with me!* *This. Is. Not. Well. With. My. Soul.*

But...it will be.

Read Psalm 34:1-3 and write the verses here: _____

_____
_____
_____
_____
_____

Oh, magnify the LORD with me, and let us exalt His name together. I encourage you to take 15-20 minutes, go to a quiet room, turn on some worship, and truly spend some time magnifying the LORD and exalting His name. If you aren't currently going through a trial or struggling with an issue, intercede for a friend or family member who is. Then write them a note telling them how you prayed for them specifically. Because the encouragement of a friend pushes a struggling faith.

TREASURES *of* DARKNESS

WEEK 9: SOVEREIGNTY

- DAY 4 -

You've almost made it. Welcome to day 44 of our 45-day study. When Moses came down from Mt. Sinai and his face shone from speaking with the LORD, it did so after just 40 days. I wish I could see your face. You probably don't know it's shining. Moses didn't. But I'd be willing to bet everyone around you sees it.

We're going to start our time together with the Amplified version of Romans 8:28 (you can find it on biblegateway.com). Look up the verse and then write it here: _____

_____

_____

_____

He works everything together. Every. Single. Thing. Fitting into a plan. For good. To and for those who love Him. There's another verse that talks about His plans. It's a popular one.

Read Jeremiah 29:11 and write the verse here: _____

_____

He knows His plan and purpose and the thoughts He thinks towards you. (Those thoughts, by the way, cannot be counted back to Him in order. They are more than can be numbered. Psalm 40:5). Remember last week when we talked about weaving our robes? The Hebrew word for "think" paints a word picture describing a weaver mixing threads and colors. He lays out the plan and picks out the thread. Colors and textures of safety and welfare, health and contentment and peace from war; not thread carrying misery, pain, or unhappiness. Sure, those things are part of our story. But they aren't our identity.

This next part is where I think most people miss the heart of Jeremiah's words. He's not making plans for the hope of your future career. Or family. Or dreams. Or livelihood. Just like the tough things in life, those are all also part of our story - but it's not what Jeremiah is referring to. Rather, he is speaking of God picking out the perfectly tailored mix of threads and colors, custom to your life. Your story. That, woven together, give you hope. And an expectation only He has. Because He sees the end from the beginning.

He knows how our robes will look when we stand before Him.

The cross-reference tucked into the Hebrew definition of that expected end is Joshua 2:18, 21. Specifically, the scarlet thread Rahab was instructed to hang in her window that would save her and her entire family.

And the expected end He's carefully picking out for us? It's referring to the latter part. The end of our lives.

Hope for heaven.

I'm going to end with an excerpt from Jesus Calling - a devotional written as if Jesus Himself were speaking to you.

"Make friends with the problems in your life. Though many things feel random and wrong, remember that I am sovereign over everything. I can fit everything into a pattern for good, but only to the extent that you trust Me. Every problem can teach you something, transforming you little by little into the masterpiece I created you to be. The very same problem can become a stumbling blog over which you fall, if you react with distrust and defiance. The choice is up to you, and you will have to choose many times each day whether to trust Me or defy Me.

The best way to befriend your problems is to thank Me for them. This simple act opens your mind to the possibility of benefits flowing from your difficulties. You can even give persistent problems nicknames, helping you to approach them with familiarity rather than dread. The next step is to introduce them to Me, enabling Me to embrace them in My loving Presence. I will not necessarily remove your problems, but My wisdom is sufficient to bring good out of every one of them."[1]

End your time today by embracing His sovereignty with thankfulness. Spending time in prayer over the problems troubling you. Big or small. And if you're not troubled, spend time in thanksgiving over all the blessings you've been entrusted with. Because He is sovereign over all - the good *and* the bad.

---

[1] *Sarah Young, Jesus Calling (Thomas Nelson, 2004), March 5.*

TREASURES *of* DARKNESS

WEEK 9: SOVEREIGNTY

- DAY 5 -

Whew. You made it. You jumped into the deep end with me and kept your head above water. From the bttom of my heart, *thank you* so much for embarking on this journey with me. I can't tell you what it means to me.

These last nine weeks have been an intensive look at some really tough things. And while it's important to understand them and use them to cultivate habits that will help us embrace trials, tribulations, and afflictions when they *do* come (because they will), it's also important to look at the incredible blessings He gives. Because He is sovereign over tragedy and hardship. But He is also sovereign over gifts and blessings.

I started this study telling you about my study on the book of Job. Searching for answers to the age old question of why bad things happen to good people. Why life seems so out of control. But as I approached the end of the book, my heart began changing. Suddenly, I recognized just how purposeful God is. And just how closely He was paying attention. *God commands the ocean to stay in its bed and the beaches of the sand hold it within its borders.*[1] He hung the galaxies and appointed the stars. He is omnipotent. All-wise and all-knowing. His judgements are true and just, even if they are mysterious. No plans of His can ever be thwarted or frustrated.

I began my summer studying Job, wanting answers. I began fall understanding that I don't deserve anything and it's by His absolute grace that there's safety and health and contentment and peace *coupled with the pain* - not just pain alone.

"We all go through stormy times in life. We all suffer pain and loss. But if we learn the lessons of our pain, if we learn to trust the wisdom and love of God, then we will come through it with our souls intact, with our lives blessed with peace, fragrance, and beauty. That is the lesson of the suffering, restoration, and peaceful passing of Job into life everlasting. ... It's a weak faith that only serves God in times of blessing. The book of Job teaches us that true faith, genuine faith, great faith is revealed only when we serve and trust God in the hard times, the times of suffering, loss, and opposition. That's the kind of faith that makes the world sit up and take notice. [Job] trembles, he falters, he questions, he pleads with God - **but he never lets go of God***. The greatest faith is that which is demonstrated when we feel the least faithful, when we feel so weak we can't do anything but cling by our fingernails."* [1]

The fact is: there is a season for joy and a season for pain. And God still reigns supreme in both. Today, I don't want to facilitate an in-depth study. Today, I want you to simply write the following verses down, and rejoice in the fact that God is a good, sovereign, *loving* God Who adores giving gifts to His children.

---

[1] Ray Stedman, *Let God Be God: Life-Changing Truths from the Book of Job* (Discovery House Publishers, 2007)

Matthew 7:9-11

Ephesians 1:3

Ephesians 4:7

James 1:17:

I've put a lot of emphasis on prayer at the end of each day throughout this study, but I think that's really the only way we can understand the sovereignty and ultimate supremacy of God. Rather than relying on the words of others, be still and hear what God wants to say to you. And turn all of these blessings into prayers of adoration for our sovereignly providential King of Kings. Every good gift comes from Him. Every perfect gift comes from Him. And we aren't deserving of any of it.

God thank You that Your strength, love, and grace are present in all circumstances - even in the worst life has to throw at us. And thank You, God, that Your character never changes. Ever. It's so easy to think things aren't lining up in my own frustration and limited perspective but You are unchanging.

You are Who You say You are. Always.
You maintain sovereign control of the universe.
You never test me beyond what I can bear.
You are patient, forgiving, and ultimately responsible for everything that happens in my life.

Thank You, God, for the privilege of infertility. Thank You, God, for the book of Job. Thank You for giving the treasures of darkness, and hidden riches of secret places, that I may know that You, the LORD, who call me by my name, are the LORD, and there is no other.

Amen.

There's just one thing left to do.

NOW THAT YOU'RE FINISHED...

How did God show up for you? What ways did you expect? In what way did He surprise you? How are you leaving this study changed? Take a minute to reflect on these last nine weeks and record the change He's effected in you through them.

Made in the
USA
Columbia, SC